just
start
now

just start now

Unlock your entrepreneur mindset and grow your wellness business

Vicky Shilling

A CIP catalogue record for this book is
available from the British Library.

ISBN 978-1-7398925-0-0

Edited by Erin Chamberlain
Design by Goldust Design
Proofread by Mary Davis Editing

For my mum.

Who made me a Just Start Now
kind of person.

Extra resources

To access resources that accompany the book
scan this QR code or go to:

https://juststartnowbook.vickyshilling.com

Contents

Introduction

"Why can't you just start now?"

"Why would anyone hire you? Can't they just do it for themselves?"

This was a question my mother posed to me in the early days of my coaching business.

And it stung.

It was summer and I'd made the journey back home to visit my family, something I did infrequently having moved to Ireland the year before to live with my boyfriend, then fiancé and now husband.

My mum lives in a rural part of South East England, Kent, in the United Kingdom. Full of pretty little houses on rambling roads through the countryside, we'd gone to a small village with a favourite restaurant of hers where we were sitting together eating a fish and chip lunch when she asked me these penetrating questions.

Her words really hit me. I was just getting started in business myself, I wasn't exactly awash with clients yet. I was trying to explain to her what it was I was doing to make money now, given I had left behind the career I had spent 10 years building in the classical music industry, something she knew far more about as a musician herself. I was now going to be helping health practitioners take action to market and sell themselves and get booked up with clients.

"But you just get on and do things if you want to do them. Why can't everyone else?"

Her line of questioning was profound. Why would anyone hire me? That sort of doubt is often the voice of my inner critic in those dark moments when I wonder what the hell I am doing mentoring wellness business owners and whether it's worthwhile at all, or if I'm just making the whole thing up.

"Why can't you just start now?" has become the question I am completely obsessed with answering. And the purpose that drives me to keep showing up and helping people entering the world of health entrepreneurship.

I see, day in and day out, amazingly qualified wellness practitioners who struggle to help anyone as they simply don't have the right business know-how and mindset to turn their knowledge and expertise into income.

It might be that you're reading this and thinking, "I don't have a mindset problem, Vicky. I have a skill-set problem. I'm just not a business person. I don't know what I'm doing."

And in part, you'd be right.

You've invested in and moved through a fantastic, reputable college course and graduated with a great qualification to be an exemplary practitioner. You've emerged the other side, bright-eyed and bushy-tailed, ready to start impacting the world with all your newfound skills and knowledge.

And then it hits you.

You don't have a clue where to begin.

How the hell do you actually *get* clients?

What are the steps to getting someone to pay you?

And what are you going to sell them anyway?!

The business advice comes flooding in from all angles and you become consumed by watching what everyone else is doing and what you're being told is necessary.

I get it. On the face of it, it looks like you have a business knowledge gap.

But there are two sides to setting up a business.

1. **The practicals** Getting clear on goals, ideal customers, packaging up offers, building a website, using social media strategically and learning the art of selling.
2. **The mindset** All the blocks, limiting beliefs and stories that hang around and stop you actually doing the practical bits.

I can teach the practicals until the cows come home. I've done pretty much all of it myself. I learned, made mistakes and refined the process into the Core Content curriculum that forms the basis of my Just Start Now course and community. I love being able to break down the practical elements of business building and make it achievable and actionable for people who are new to all the concepts so they start to feel like real, fully-fledged business owners.

But it's the mindset that will make or break all the practical actions you take and determine whether this all turns into a raving success, or a whole load of time and energy for no return.

It's the mindset that really fascinates me.

It's the mindset tweaks and changes that I want to share with you here in this book.

I want to pick apart why it is that some people can throw themselves into the practical aspects of business building while others are paralysed, frozen into inaction by their own thoughts.

I want to understand why it is that some people can handle rejection, flops and failures while others live in fear of experiencing knock backs, so much so that they self-sabotage and hide, instead of taking action.

Why can't some people just 'do it for themselves' as my mother put it?

That's where coaching meets mentoring in my work.

As a mentor I can show you the tasks to do and give my advice and share my experience.

But as a coach, I need to help you identify what's stopping you, or what *will* stop you if you try between our sessions to take action.

Getting to know yourself, identifying and if necessary reprogramming the thought processes that are blocking you, is part of the 'legacy' of my work with clients. They step away from our time together telling me they have a 'little Vicky' inside their head, which leaves me feeling super proud.

That's because I don't want anyone to become reliant on me telling them what to do at every turn (the real me that is, not the little version in their head).

I want clients to come away from our time together understanding themselves and their own habits, stories and beliefs so that when they are alone with a task or decision (as we all mostly are in solopreneurship), they are able to take action without me there.

This book therefore is not another digital marketing 'how-to' guide.

It's not going to tell you how to create a funnel, what the strategies are to move people from a free Facebook group into paying customers or how to grow a social media following that buys from you. If you've picked this book up to learn that stuff, you can put it right back down now. (And head to my website instead, where I can teach you that.)

This book is a look at what stops you 'just starting now'. Digging into this is going to underline all the practical steps and knowledge you acquire as you build a business.

Throughout the chapters we will move through the mindset blocks that come up at each stage of your business set up.

Having mentored hundreds of wellness practitioners over the years, I now have a methodology for getting started which I've turned into a five pillar process.

1. **Clarity** on your goals and ideal customer.
2. **Packaging and pricing** to turn your knowledge into irresistible offers.
3. **Selling** your way. Finding a way to feel comfortable and confident promoting what you do.
4. **Your sites** are important so that you build a solid digital home in the form of a website and mailing list.
5. **Connection** so that you find customers by creating content and implementing strategies.

Each chapter will unpack and help you examine the common mindsets and beliefs that I have seen over and over again in budding wellness business owners as they progress through this framework to turn their qualifications into income.

I know you're someone with huge dreams, big capabilities, a wealth of knowledge and expertise in the sphere of health where you've dedicated yourself. I've watched and benefitted from so many people like you, which is why I'm so impassioned about helping this sector.

I came into this industry through my own health journey. Struggling with recurrent bouts of IBS (Irritable Bowel Syndrome) I felt like I'd entered another world when I started to discover the wealth of nutritionists, dietitians, health coaches, yoga teachers, personal trainers and mindfulness practitioners who were sharing their knowledge and on a mission to improve the world's health.

I could see their dedication. I was blown away by their commitment and the bold life changes many of them had made to go 'all in' on using their qualifications.

I benefitted hugely from people just like you. I learned to make adjustments to my diet, tune into my body, prioritise movement and change how I thought through listening, watching, reading, investing in and learning from experts, all with life changing results for my own health and well-being.

I was totally hooked. The impact was undeniable. And the healthy living community I became part of was full of people I wanted to see succeed.

Over time I realised the best way I could do that was not in fact to train as a practitioner myself (though I made a minor contribution to helping people with their healthy eating through my blog *The Flourishing Pantry* which is where I learned a lot of my online marketing skills!). The best way I could support those who had undergone that rigorous training was to infuse them with my 'just start now' attitude.

I know you. You don't want everything you've trained for to have just been an expensive hobby you once dabbled in but never made anything substantial from. And it breaks my heart to see that be the case for hundreds of thousands of talented and much needed practitioners.

Bringing it all together and turning what you now know into an income is terrifying and eluding you.

This book is here to help.

It's so important that you get your entrepreneur mindset set up from the very beginning. Without it, all the actions, courses, trainings and study in the world will not enable you to make the impact you want. I've seen it a hundred times over. People outwardly doing all the 'right' things. But on the inside, in their heads, completely sabotaging their ability to get results.

I'm not going to let that be you.

Before you dive in, I want to reiterate this. I'm not a psychiatrist, nor a psychology expert. I've never studied the human mind in any scholarly way and my scientific knowledge of the brain and how it works is probably laughable compared with yours. There won't be any fancy analysis here.

I also have no doubt that as I grow and develop as a coach and mentor and keep training and adding to my skills, I will learn more and more about the subconscious and the reasons *why* people do, or don't do, the things they want.

But what I do know is that having worked with and witnessed hundreds of people now setting up wellness businesses, there are many common blocks and issues that come up time and time again that I want to address and help you cast aside. Things that you might until now have believed were just you and your crazy brain, alone in the world. Things that clearly other people that look like action takers and go-getters don't suffer with.

The truth is we all suffer with these blocks.

Every single example in this book is something I have seen tens if not hundreds of people struggle with. And if I've seen hundreds, that means there are tens of thousands, if not more, out there, just like us (and yes, I include myself in struggle with many of these mindset blocks!). The only difference between the ones who make it and the ones that don't is how they react and move forward in the face of the mindsets and limiting beliefs that might otherwise hold them back.

I want you to be one of the ones who can master their mindset and take action right now. Again and again. Every day. Until you get the outcome you desire.

By the end of this book I want you to feel you're an "I can just get on and do this if I want it" person (as my mother so perfectly said it). Because you'll have identified and learned to reprogramme the habits, stories and fixed mindsets that are currently getting in your way. And you'll truly know that the inner critic in your head is the only barrier between you and the business you really want.

How to change your mindset

Throughout this book we'll touch on many, many fixed mindsets and limiting beliefs that are most likely going to come up for you throughout the course of starting your business.

What are fixed mindsets and limiting beliefs?

You are wildly capable. But there are thought patterns that your mind plays on repeat that hold you back from fulfilling your potential.

A fixed mindset is a belief that you are bad at something based on your inherent nature and are incapable of change. "I'm not good at sales" or "I'm useless with technology", for example.

Limiting beliefs are thoughts and opinions that you believe to be the truth that stop you moving forward.

Many are formed in childhood and might be things like "I'm not good enough", "work has to be hard", or "people like me don't make great money".

Some of these fixed mindsets or limiting beliefs you'll already be aware of – they're the big hairy stories and fears that loom large when you think about doing something bold, like starting a website or posting some tips on social media. BOOM. There they are. Staring you down. Stopping you in your tracks.

Some of them you're not even aware of yet. But you soon will be as you work your way through these pages. Sorry about that! #SorryNotSorry actually. I'm not sorry because I want this to be a comprehensive handbook for you to turn to whenever a new mindset blocks pop up for you throughout your first few years of business.

Doing it this way, with every possible mindset issue laid out now, means you know you've got the toolkit, the examples, and the reassurance that whenever it comes up for you, this new fear is totally normal and you are absolutely able to overcome it too.

In 2017 I quit my job in the music industry and moved to Ireland. I used this as my opportunity for a fresh start – to reinvent what I did for work and to leverage the connections I'd gained from the healthy eating food blog I'd built up and to start earning money in a new way.

But boy, did I have fixed mindsets and limiting beliefs about making that possible. I didn't have entrepreneur parents like many who make it going solo, so I'd never learned the best way to think when you're running your own business. I carried with me the fixed mindsets and limiting beliefs that had seeped in from growing up in a single parent family, being a good girl academic and diligent PAYE employee.

Mornings were always worst for me when I started my business. Waking up first thing, those stories and negative thoughts were always at their loudest.

> This is never going to work
> You need to get a real job
> Who's going to pay you?
> You'll never have any money
> You're not good enough to do this

Maybe you can relate.

I knew it needed to change. I knew thinking like this wasn't helpful or healthy. But how?

Changing the language you use in your head, the fears that plague you and the actions you habitually take (or don't take), does not happen overnight.

Just like you when it comes to changing your clients' health, I do not have a magic weight-loss lolly, miracle cure juice or fast-track training plan to change the way you think in an instant.

It's the thing my clients most often bemoan when we've worked out what's blocking them.

"How can I stop thinking like this?!"

In my own experience, and that of the clients I've worked with, changing how you think takes time. And that makes sense, right? Because usually the thought patterns we need to unpick are ones that we've had for years and years. Sometimes decades. So the idea we can just click our fingers and POOF! we don't think like that anymore . . . That doesn't make sense.

In order to effect long-term change on where my brain wandered off to when I was tackling my business building journey, I took the following steps and I'd recommend you give them a go too.

> **Notice**
> **Stay non-judgemental**
> **Be kind**
> **Apply some logic**
> **Neutralise or flip**
> **Repeat, repeat, repeat**

Notice

The first step to changing how you think is to notice how you're currently thinking. You can't change the words going on in there if you don't first really tune in to the ones you're using right now.

The best advice I can give you to be able to stop and notice what you're subconsciously saying to yourself is to use a health and wellness staple: meditation.

For me, regular meditation (and I'm not talking anything major – just five to ten minutes a day) gave me the ability to really hear my own inner critic. The practice helped me notice the negative and unhelpful thoughts as they came and went and identify that they weren't really 'me' at all. They were just words. Thoughts. Things that popped up and floated past. They came. And they went.

Not sure what I mean about harnessing meditation to get better at noticing your thoughts? Let me get an expert to explain.

Here's Laura Farrington, fully qualified yoga and meditation teacher and founder of Meditate With Laura:

"The most common misconception about meditation is that we are trying to clear the mind of thought. This is 100% incorrect. We are always thinking about something, even when we are thinking about the breath . . . that in itself is a thought! We are thinking machines, it's in our makeup, we even think when we sleep.

It's no wonder most people give up on meditation so fast. If your belief is that we are here to clear the mind of thoughts then that's never going to happen which is why most people presume meditation isn't working for them.

Meditation is simply Awareness. Awareness of what we are thinking and why we think that way. It is Awareness of our thought patterns. These thought patterns will be different for everyone based on their life experience.

When we take five to ten minutes every day to be still and observe our thoughts we come to realise that a lot of our thinking is irrational and fear-based. We come to realise that the way we speak to ourselves can be harmful and not conducive to us living our best lives.

The more you meditate the more you realise that the past is in the past. The future has not yet happened yet the present moment is all we have. The here and now.

Once you become aware of what you're thinking and how you speak to yourself you can start to say better things to yourself like:

I am capable

I am strong

I am fit and healthy

I am enough

These new more positive thoughts will eventually get embedded into your subconscious and you begin to live by them. Awareness of how you think and why you think that way, will change your life for the better forever." [1]

For me when I'm meditating, in that stillness, I can start to hear the words my mind says to me as sentences, phrases and statements. I am genuinely listening and observing my own mind and what it's saying, instead of being overwhelmed and caught up in the feelings they create when I 'hear' them on the go, in the midst of doing something in my life or business.

When I first started tuning in like this, the negative statements I had on repeat in my mind when I was getting started were:

> ❯ This will never work
> ❯ You're always running out of money
> ❯ Who wants to listen to you?

Do they resonate?

Being able to identify these through mindfully observing my thoughts gives me the power to remove them. But first . . .

Stay non-judgemental

It is essential once you've identified what your mind is saying to you that's holding you back, that you don't become angry at yourself.

It's a somewhat natural reaction of course – when we're solo business building we can point the finger at no one else. So it's immensely frustrating to learn that we're sabotaging ourselves simply by repeatedly saying all the wrong things, out loud or in our heads.

When you identify your limiting belief, you might think:

> ❯ I'm such an idiot for thinking this
> ❯ I'm so sick of hearing myself say this!
> ❯ This is such a stupid thing to think

I know on those mornings when that voice was loud and cruel I felt incredibly frustrated at myself. But please, try to refrain from this kind of abuse. You wouldn't say it to a friend!

Instead, notice your thoughts completely without judgement. For those familiar with meditation, you'll know this is an extension of the practice after we observe our thoughts.

Laura Farrington explains for us again how this works:

"In meditation, there is an exercise called 'witnessing and labelling your thoughts'.

For example, as you meditate you may notice you're thinking about what to have for breakfast. That would be labelled as a 'future thought'.

Then you may notice you are thinking about a co-worker that frustrated you in the past so we label that a 'thought from the past'.

And then you notice you're thinking about your new business venture and we label that a 'happy thought'.

No matter what kind of thoughts, feelings or bodily sensations come up as you meditate, we are taught to be the witness to them all, to be a neutral observer to what arises. Detaching from what your mind says and does enables you to find more calm, peace, and positivity. Take your power back and practise this daily!"

When my negative stories are visible to me, I like to replace the potential angry phrases I could default to, with non-judgemental things such as:

> ❯ Oh look! That's where my mind has gone!
> ❯ Isn't that interesting . . . that's coming up for me again
> ❯ Wow, I didn't expect that to pop up here

Neutral. Non-judgemental. Can you do the same for yours?

Be kind

As we've already touched on, some of the thoughts you'll have towards yourself when you realise the negative rubbish going on in your head will be some pretty harsh ones, words you would never use when talking to someone else.

It's imperative that as well as staying neutral about it, that we show ourselves some kindness for having these thoughts.

Firstly, because slagging ourselves off has *never* got long-lasting, positive results. Just as hating your body into losing weight doesn't work, hating your mind into being an entrepreneurial thinker is not going to pan out well either.

And secondly, because any inner critic thoughts really come from a place of survival. They come from your mind trying to ensure you stay safe, stay accepted and stay inside the group.

And, at the end of the day, that's a *kind* thing to be doing. That voice in a lot of other instances is literally saving your ass and keeping you alive. Helping you make decisions on a daily basis that allow you to exist into the next day.

It's normal for your mind to think these things. It wants to find the path of least resistance to ensure you stay breathing. So doing brave, bold, new things that might risk your existence are all things it's going to try and sabotage, in whatever way it can.

Be kind to yourself.

This is normal.

The way you're thinking is normal.

Your mind is trying to keep you safe.

Be grateful you have a mind that wants you to stay alive.

But we can't let safety and security and playing small win every time. Or we'd never get anything done.

So it's time to . . .

Apply some logic

Now we've got a phrase or a statement to work with. It's a set of words that you've realised is infinitely unhelpful to your business-building ambitions – and one we've detached from emotionally and been kind to ourselves about for thinking it.

The next step is to apply some logic to it. That's because we need to take the power out of it. Bring that thought down a peg or two.

For example: let's take my inner critic's firm favourite when I was a new business owner: "This will never work."

We can apply some logic.

> What evidence do you have that this won't work?
> What evidence do you have that this *will* work?
> Has nothing you've done before ever worked out?
> What will happen if it doesn't work?

Coming from a non-judgemental, kind, noticing space, applying some gentle logical questions to our statement starts to knock the wind out of its sails.

Rather than spinning off from a negative thought into negative feelings that cause negative actions, we can pause and prevent that cycle by apply logic.

When I apply this logic to my 'This will never work' inner critic voice, I start to realise that the statement is far from reality.

Staring myself back in the mirror in the mornings, I would work through this process and gradually, calmly and kindly point out to myself that there were plenty of people that *were* making it work, which was all the evidence I needed that I could do it too.

Neutralise or flip

Now we've applied some logic we know that this statement, this 'fact', really isn't the truth.

So we need to replace it. With something more helpful and more in line with the truth we know and want to experience.

This replacement is essential! Just like any bad habit, like smoking or picking your nails, all the advice on changing these long term involve a replacement habit.

Same goes for your brain.

Don't leave it hanging. Because it will just default to one of its regular negative tropes unless you give it something else to get its teeth into.

There are two ways you can replace a negative thought pattern, and they're dependent on where you're at in your mind.

The most powerful thing you can do with a negative statement is flip it. Give it a 180° treatment and state something in the affirmative that completely counters and contradicts that nagging, negative self-talk that keeps coming up for you.

> This will never work
> *becomes*
> Things are always working out for me
> You're always running out of money
> *becomes*
> I always have money
> Who wants to listen to you?
> *becomes*
> People love listening to what I have to say

However, the key with the 180° flip is **you need to believe the new statement.** There is no point putting in a replacement that feels like bullsh*t to you.

This is where, for me, picking lavish affirmations about luxury, wealth and abundance off a Pinterest board and repeating them every day, is never going to have an effect.

We've all met those people. They seem to be living in cloud cuckoo land, without a grip on reality. What comes out of their mouth doesn't seem to draw any parallels to their actions or life.

For this process to work you've got to be fully subscribed to what you're saying.

If a full, 180°, super positive statement just is *not* something you can convince yourself of (and there is no shame in that – as we've said, changing mindsets takes time), then you need to neutralise.

Remember what your mother used to say?

"If you can't say something nice, say something neutral instead."

Okay, she didn't quite say that, but let's go with it.

> This will never work
> *becomes*
> Things can work out for me
> You're always running out of money
> *becomes*
> I am getting better with money every day
> Who wants to listen to you?
> *becomes*
> I am building an audience that love what I do

Whichever way you choose to do it, you need to come up with alternative statements, words and phrases that eliminate your trash talk.

You won't be able to do this all in one go. You're going to have to identify these negative thoughts and come up with your alternatives as they arise. You won't just sit down one day and remember all your harmful self-talk in one sitting.

Instead you'll notice the negative thoughts in the moment they hit you, or while you're meditating, or as you're falling asleep at night. So you'll need to be prepared to notice and neutralise or flip them.

I'd recommend keeping a note on your phone or a page in a notebook where you start to work these out and collect them. Because once you've got new statements that are much healthier for your entrepreneur mindset you need to . . .

Repeat, repeat, repeat

Once you have these new statements you've got to start embedding them. And they need to be embedded as deeply as their previous incarnations were buried. Deep in the subconscious where they can start to work their magic.

And to get in there we have to be clever and repetitive. Really repetitive.

My tried and tested ways to get these new phrases into my subconscious are:

> Saving them as my phone lock screen
> Saving them on my computer desktop
> Sticking them on Post-its in places where I'll see them daily
> Recording myself saying them in a voice memo on my phone, and then listening to them whilst on

walks (I did a mix of 10–15 affirmations in one recording, not the same one over and over)
› Saving them in my phone as a reminder to show up at random intervals during the week

For example I started this chapter stating "you are wildly capable". That's a phrase I embedded in my mind by having it as the screensaver on my phone for two months so I saw it every day. And now it's stuck.

Some people might say read them out loud to yourself in the mirror. That's one step too far for me personally. But go for it if that feels right for you!

Whichever method you choose (and I'd recommend implementing multiple ones simultaneously), stick with it for as long as it takes for that new phrase to sink in.

How do you know when it has?

It will randomly start popping up in your conversations and thoughts without you even realising.

For example, one of the new more positive money mindsets I wanted to embed was "money comes in expected and unexpected ways". This was one I had programmed as a reminder in my phone and also one I listened to myself saying, among others, when I popped to the shops every day.

And slowly but surely it became part of what I said to myself and others. It felt like the *totally* natural thing to say to clients at certain points in our conversations. I'd suddenly get an offer of work or a speaking engagement I wasn't expecting – and this new phrase was the logical thing to say in acknowledgement. I'd be talking to a business bestie who tells me about a windfall inheritance they came into. My new phrase is the perfect way to respond to them.

It's now one of my firm favourites and where my brain naturally goes to when thinking about making money, instead of the old, tired, negative stories. All through repeating it and dropping it into my brain over and over.

Won't this take forever, Vicky?

Now this process might sound long-winded. And yes, initially it will take time because you're not used to doing it.

Like anything new, it will feel clunky, forced and hard work. Exhausting sometimes even, to feel you're fighting to change your mindset.

I've been there. For me in those early days it genuinely felt like a battle that would never end trying to stamp out these old ways of thinking.

Every day the same: Spot the thought. Try to not get angry. Notice. Observe. Apply logic. Neutralise or flip.

And repeat.

Over and over.

So yes, it will take time. Sometimes weeks, sometimes months, sometimes maybe years.

But trust me, this process works. And it's so worth it.

When you have the ability to change your thoughts, things suddenly feel possible for you. I can confidently say that using this technique with many, many of my own negative thought patterns I now:

> Feel more positive about money
> Believe that I can attract ideal clients
> Keep showing up even if it feels like no one is listening
> Charge what I'm worth
> Know that I am deserving of what I want in life

The language doesn't change the circumstances we find ourselves in, of course. A recession, a family illness, a crappy boss, a global pandemic, tumbleweed on our latest social media post, a flop of a launch, a discovery call that doesn't convert.

But it changes what we believe, feel, know and do when we're faced with those situations. And that's what gets results.

Limiting belief whack-a-mole

One thing to point out is that you won't ever 'complete' your mindset. It's not like a computer game or a digital course. You won't have ever nailed everything that holds you back inside that head of yours.

I'd love to say that I *only* ever now think that money comes in expected and unexpected ways, all day every day.

But I get bad days too. Those really deep-rooted stories are tough to shift completely.

And that's because one of the inner critic's most clever tricks is to present you with new reincarnated versions of previous fears you thought you'd quashed.

Unhelpfully, your fears and doubts can rear their heads in a new form just to keep you small. I affectionately call this 'limiting belief whack-a-mole'. Remember that game you had as a kid?

Just when you think you've bopped one mole (read: limiting belief) on the head for good, it'll reappear somewhere else in a new guise and you need to be ready for it.

With your hammer. With your tool kit.

Notice. Be kind. Apply the logic. Flip it.

Repeat. Repeat. Repeat.

It's worth it.

Give it a go.

With any mindset block you identify that comes up in this book, in order to change it, take it through these stages:

Notice

Stay non-judgemental

Be kind

Apply some logic

Neutralise or flip

Repeat, repeat, repeat

I'll help you through it and offer you logic and flips throughout. Let's change your mind about becoming a business owner.

1

Why you need to set goals and yet you don't

When I work with entrepreneurs who want to build their wellness business we always start at the same place.

Goal setting.

Clarity on where you're aiming to be in one year's time, five years' time or 10 years' time – that big vision – is what helps determine the actions you should take.

It also helps you avoid the treacherous 'shiny object syndrome' of watching other business owners do the latest cool and exciting thing that you think you need to jump on.

Goal setting is like using Google Maps. If you don't know where you're heading, the route is impossible to plot. And when the route is impossible to see, you end up taking random detours and jumping from one path to the next, without actually doing things that are purposeful and move you towards the end result *you* want.

You'll be busy, yes. But totally and utterly unfulfilled, and never reaching your destination. Because you haven't set one.

Despite this perfectly logical explanation for why goal setting is effective – and I have absolutely no doubt you're nodding along to as you read this chapter – most people don't set any goals at all. Do you?

If the answer is no, you may be one of the many people I've encountered that avoid goal setting at every turn with a myriad of reasons for why it doesn't, or won't, work for them.

I've heard pretty much all the excuses for not goal setting under the sun by now. And I think they boil down to three fundamental reasons:

1. You're afraid of failure
2. You're afraid of success
3. You're not allowing yourself to dream

You're afraid of failure

A classic fear. When I ask clients why they don't like setting goals, they say things such as:

> I've tried it before, but I just felt so awful when I didn't reach them

> ❯ I find setting goals is demoralising, because I know I won't make them
> ❯ What I want just feels totally unachievable, what's the point of even writing it down?

Writing down goals brings up a lot of doubts and worries about not achieving the goal and what that means. Or more accurately what you *make it mean*.

Let's unpick that.

I definitely had a fear of failure when I started my business. I'm a straight-A, first-class degree, need-to-get-it-right-and-never-look-stupid kinda gal. I went to a girls grammar school and was in a fiercely competitive (in a friendly way!) class with other high achievers. Getting it wrong or flunking a test just wasn't something we did.

Being open to not hitting the goals I set myself in my business was a massive lesson I had to learn and get comfortable with.

For example, when I started my business I set myself financial goals for the first three months I went totally solo. €250 for January, €750 for February and €1,200 for March. I wanted to start off small and 'achievable' (whatever that even means).

The first month I achieved my teeny tiny goal! Hooray! I booked a one-to-one client and got asked to build a website for a brand I loved. Smashed it! This is going to work.

Then February came. And went. I got a couple of other one-off bookings, but I didn't hit my target. I made

€500, some way off the €750 target.

Eek. Okay . . . well maybe March will be better? Maybe I'll make up the money I didn't achieve in February then? I'll roll the income goals together and work even harder in March . . .

I'll be honest, I did really start to wobble at this point. Failure wasn't in my vocabulary. I met up with a fellow coach and talked about how hard I was finding the financial target. It had become a stick to beat myself with and it seemed to be falling further and further out of reach. Could I focus on how many clients I was getting, instead of the income, she suggested?

But nope. Whichever way I looked at it, things were starting to tumble. March was an even bigger goal and I was even further away from reaching that by the time I checked in and looked at my numbers at the end of the month.

Gulp. My financial goal for the year looked like it was slipping away with each month that passed. I had a choice at this point:

1. To read the numbers and interpret the figures as a sign that I was doomed and this was never going to work.
   Or
2. To read the numbers and interpret the figures as a sign that I was growing and making progress – that while it wasn't what I had projected or hoped, it was moving in the right direction.

Because not achieving a goal is, in itself, just a fact.

I set a goal. I didn't reach it.

Fact.

Not achieving a goal doesn't have to mean that *you're* a failure, that you're crap at this, that it will never work, that you're useless at setting goals, or whatever other story you've attached to it. That's just what you're choosing to make it mean – subconsciously of course; no one would actively *choose* to feel like this.

What do you make it mean when you 'fail' to reach a goal? What does that little voice inside your head tell you?

Because that voice? *You* get to decide what it says to you.

I stopped being afraid of setting goals when I stopped letting that voice in my head tell me all the negative stories about who I was and what I was not capable of if I didn't achieve them. And I started to let go of whether the outcome I wrote down happened or not.

SAY WHAT?

Yes, I'll repeat that.

I let go . . . released . . . stopped focusing on . . . whether I hit the goal or not.

Instead, when I set goals and reflected on whether I did or didn't reach them, **I focused on what I learned and who I became along the way** as I was pursuing that goal.

In my first year earning in my business I wrote down that I wanted to earn €40,000. I broke my goal down month by month and kept an eye on whether I hit my monthly targets.

Did I make that goal for the year? No.

I made €22,000 that year.

Did I make that mean I was a failure? That I was crap? That I'd never set a goal again?

Nope. I *chose* to think differently about it.

What I made it mean was that I showed up. That I had proved to myself I can make money from doing this. That I had stepped out of my comfort zone. That I learned a heap from even daring to write that goal, break it down and work towards the monthly targets. That everything I had done that year was laying the groundwork for the next year. That nothing was wasted.

I silenced (okay, quietened) the voice that told me it meant all these negative things about me, my prospects and my business – and chose to tune in instead to a voice that told me progress of any kind was positive.

So if you're afraid of failure when it comes to setting goals, ask yourself these questions.

"What am I making it mean if I fail to reach my goal?"

"Can I change what I think about the outcome?"

You're afraid of success

Before I start working with anyone one-to-one I always arrange a discovery call. I want to know if they're a good fit for the sort of support I offer and if I am the right person to help them.

Niamh was one such client. Trained as a health coach and wanting to step away from a stressful full-time career as a pharmacist, our work together would be focused on creating an audience and solid grounding for her to pivot into health coaching part-time, a job she could do on her own terms.

"How exciting," I said. "Paint the picture for me, Niamh – if we were to work together and get everything sorted for your health coaching business, tell me how things would look in 12 months' time."

For some this is an exciting exercise. But as Niamh started to share how that future would look, her fears and doubts started to show.

As I asked her these questions.

"What if this goes well?"

"What if it works out?"

"What if you get fully booked?"

"What if you make loads of money? "

Niamh's mind gave the only answer it could using the evidence from her life to date. Burn-out.

"If I build this business and get busy, I'm scared I'll hate it and get burned out all over again," she said.

"I can't imagine a business that gives me a life where I actually have balance, because I've never had that."

"I'm scared if it all goes really well I might not be able to cope and keep up."

The bigger, underlying fear when it comes to setting goals that I see time and time again is actually the *opposite* of failure.

When we really probe into what's going on if you aren't taking action, like Niamh, it might just be because you're terrified that doing all this work will wind you right back at the same place you're trying to get away from now – total and utter exhaustion. A place where you can't keep up with demand. Where you struggle to get enough sleep. Where you have to work all hours available and miss out on time with your family and friends.

A life characterised by burn-out is the exact opposite of what you want to achieve setting up your own business. Because, overwhelmingly, people starting their own wellness business have been on their own journey to move away from a life that leaves them feeling tired and drained.

Maybe, like Niamh, you've come to your new business via a corporate career – and it's left you exhausted. So now, with a newfound understanding and training in health and wellness, you want to live a life that feels more aligned with your values and allows you to prioritise and care for your well-being.

As a result, when you emerge from your practitioner training, raring to go to help both your clients and yourself live a healthier, happier, more balanced life, you're faced with two demons.

1. Hustle culture

The more coaches and business content creators you follow online, the more you get the vibe that you need to work crazy hard, put the hours in, do whatever it takes, succeed at all costs. The people making the sort of money you want are making it look pretty gruelling to achieve. Is it even possible to do this for a job *and* feel more at peace, or is it just a pipe dream?

2. Your deep-rooted corporate mentality

You might not even notice it, but you very likely believe that the only way to make money and be successful is to work longer hours, take on all the clients and do things that make you feel uncomfortable, just to get the results you want. And that's perfectly understandable. Because that's what you've done so far to bring home the bacon.

Both these voices are telling you a simple (inaccurate!) formula.

More hours + more stress + hustling hard = success (money, flexibility, freedom, dream work)

You won't set, and feel great about, goals if you think that doing so will lead to burn-out. You will only continue to self-sabotage and get in your own way if you think that on the other side of results is a miserable life that you don't want to live.

Read that again.

You won't set, and feel great about, goals if you think that doing so will lead to burn-out.

You need to shake off those fears of getting exhausted and overwhelmed and fully trust that setting goals and striving to reach them is going to lead to an amazing life that surpasses all your expectations.

You need to fully believe that you will be in control of your workload, how you market yourself and what your average week will look like. Then you can curate it in a way that feels really exciting and rewarding – and that gives you all the freedom and flexibility you want.

Do you believe that?

Because if not, this leads me nicely onto . . .

You're not allowing yourself to dream

I used to run wellness retreats for women. One of the first weekend events we ran involved a goal-setting exercise which came after reviewing the well-known coaching exercise, the wheel of life[2]. Picture a big dining table in a gorgeous period estate in the Irish midlands countryside. Each attendee had assessed the wheel to see which areas of their life they felt had been neglected and need focus going forward.

In order to come up with a plan, we asked them to first dream big and write down what a 'ten out of ten' would look and feel like in this particular area of their life. For example, if they'd realised that their environment needed their attention, we asked them to imagine and describe their dream home or office, or a gorgeous new bedroom revamp.

As we sat in silence and allowed the women to write, one let out a sigh.

"This is all well and good but it's not very realistic is it?" she complained. "I mean, I can write down that I want to be a millionaire and live in a mansion in a hot country, but it's not going to actually happen. Surely I should be more reasonable with what I'm putting down, don't you think?"

Realistic. Reasonable. Pragmatic. Level-headed. Rational.

Whatever it is you want to call it.

We have a tendency to shut ourselves and our thoughts down rather than opening up to possibilities and thinking bigger.

Maybe that's the case for you if you struggle to set yourself goals: You're not letting yourself really go there. You've blocked your ability to imagine, visualise and truly immerse yourself in what life could be like if you achieved what you want.

You've stuffed up your ability to dream with focusing only on what's 'achievable' and 'realistic'. And that's not your fault. After all, that's what SMART goals are, right? Achievable/Attainable, Realistic – just some of the words used for the A and R in the acronym.

But this attachment to only setting and speaking goals that are achievable, attainable and realistic is strangling your ability to dream bigger.

An all-too-common answer when I ask people what they want (which is the *classic* coaching question by the way, from which all other questions follow) is "I don't know."

"I don't know" usually really means one of the following things:

> ❯ I don't feel worthy to have the things I want
> ❯ I'm scared I'm going to be judged for speaking out loud the things I want
> ❯ I worry I'll become a horrible person if I get everything I want
> ❯ I feel limited by things that have happened in the past and so I don't truly believe it's possible to have what I want
> ❯ I can't see the path to *how* I get what I want, so it's pointless dreaming

This last one has been a big one for me. I am not a natural dreamer. The 'how' always gets in the way.

When I trained as a coach we were given a tool called the Disney Method. We were taught Walt Disney had his offices divided into three distinct groups of people – the dreamers, the realists and the critics.

The dreamers came up with the crazy big ideas. The realists looked at *how* to make the ideas happen. The critics would point out flaws and problems in the plan. The concept was that the dreamers passed down the big idea, and then the realists and critics would circulate and workshop the idea until it turned into a workable plan.

We all have the ability to step into each of these roles in our heads, but one role might come more naturally than the others.

As we practised using this tool I was fascinated by the clear division between the dreamers and the realists in our group.

47

The dreamers could happily spend large sections of their sample coaching session visualising how they wanted things to be. They relished being in that space as they created a vivid image of what things would be like in their dream scenario.

But me? I struggled to be the dreamer. If I allowed myself to go there even for a second I'd immediately go into realist mode. But *how* was that going to be possible?

We all have dreams. Even if they're buried deep down and not often visited, they're in there. The real 'you' knows what you truly desire.

It's usually just that one of the limiting thoughts I've listed above (or maybe a new one I haven't heard before – I'm open to a different version for my limiting beliefs whack-a-mole game!) is stopping you from letting that part of your mind go to town and paint that vivid picture. You shut it down. You think it's ridiculous to even let your mind wander that way.

Who am I to imagine a dream life?

Who am I to have a life that allows me to do what I love and earn money?

Who am I to get what I want when so many others don't?

Stop right there!

Let's reframe.

A better question would be: who are you *not* to imagine a dream life for yourself?

Because here's the thing:

You were born worthy.

You. Are. Worthy.

Always have been. Always will be.

And as a result of being fabulously worthy, you deserve to have everything you want.

Write that down somewhere you'll see it every day. It's the truth.

I'll say it again for good measure.

You. Are. Worthy.

Always have been. Always will be.

There doesn't need to be a reason. You don't have to have earned it. You don't have to sacrifice something in order to achieve it. Achieving it doesn't deprive someone else of what they want (we're going to talk a lot more about this when it comes to pricing in Chapter 6).

You're allowed to want what you want and have it.

Just because.

Sit with that.

I have had to spend a lot of time working on this myself and finding ways to open up and imagine without limits. How? By spending time with dreamers to inspire me and watching how their brains work, prioritising time for journaling and seeing what comes out, and planning in time each year where I stop to think big, rather than getting caught up in the day-to-day minutia (which I'd happily stay in all day, every day!).

Interestingly, that participant who complained about being asked to dream and think big for her life on our retreat? She went on to move to Australia, change her career from beautician to holistic practitioner and popped up in my Facebook group to say she'd earned her first $AUD100,000 a couple of years later. Maybe allowing her to dream *had* had a useful effect, even if she didn't think so at the time.

Let's talk about the inner critic

All of these blocks to goal setting (fear of failure, fear of success, fear to dream) are articulated by the voice of the inner critic.

The inner critic is a character that is going to crop up a lot in this book and I want to be clear about it at this early stage in our journey.

> "The Inner critic subpersonality is that critical inner voice that judges, attacks, demeans and beats us up."
>
> **Jodie Gale, Psychotherapist,**
> **counsellor and coach**[3]

The important part of this definition is the word "subpersonality". Your inner critic is a role that plays out in your mind in order to protect you and serve you or help you cope in some way.

Your inner critic voice is trying, bless it, to keep you safe. And small. And not protect you so that you don't stretch too far out of those carefully-crafted comfort zones that you've made for yourself.

It's your basic human instinct kicking in.

Keep small. Keep safe. Stay alive.

But ultimately . . . your inner critic is not you.

It's not the *real* you.

The real, true you, is the part inside you that's getting itchy and uncomfortable because it knows it's made for

51

more. The part that knows that it's got so much potential to fulfil. The part that knows that if it just applied itself and took action, it could really make waves, have an impact and get what it wants.

The real you knows with steadfast determination that it *is* capable. But the inner critic is stomping it down.

The inner critic might sometimes feel like it's become you. But that's only when you've let it rule the roost and control your actions, or more likely *inactions*, for too long.

In those instances when the inner critic has been allowed to go wild and control the show, you've lost touch with the real, confident, assured you. And you're listening instead to the doubt, judgement, criticism or demeaning things the inner critic is spouting. That could well have been happening for years.

But I promise, that's not the real you.

One way to really help you differentiate 'you' from your inner critic is to give your inner critic a name. Imagine them like a caricature with physical features and a particular voice that you can put on when they pipe up with something unhelpful or limiting.

My client Natalie is a fantastic example of someone who, through marketing her work as a life coach, pokes fun at her inner critic and really personifies it in order to differentiate it from the true her.

Natalie's social media feed is filled with photos of her dressing up as her inner critic, pulling funny faces and captioning her images with the *exact* statements and stories the critic is saying to keep her and her ideal clients small.

"What if I'm no good at a new job?"

"No one wants to see what you have to say on Instagram."

"What if I make a mistake?"

It's funny, you can't help but smile when you see the images. But whilst we can smile and laugh at her playful approach, it's also flagging something important – that this voice is not the real us and it is not telling the truth. Turning it into a comedic image and posting it in public is a great reminder (and because it resonates with her audience, it's great marketing too, by the way!).

Differentiating 'your' thoughts from the words that spring from the mouth of a nasty character can help separate and remove you from their strength inside your head.

You might even find that if you start to put a name and features to that critic it becomes a bit clearer who's voice it really is . . . a sibling perhaps? Or that nasty old boss you had once a few years back?

It's perfectly normal if your inner critic morphs into a little version of someone in your life, past or present. It all helps you realise where these stories come from. And it's not the centre of you.

Here's the thing though. Whilst I've brought this inner critic character up, I don't have the answer to removing it in this chapter. Nor any chapter of this book to be honest – but don't worry, there are lots of other reasons to keep reading!

That's because I've never come across anything in my business that has been magically fixed with a single 'ah ha!' realisation. We absolutely get those lightbulb moments where something clicks thanks to the right delivery or hearing it at the right time. But for long-term, sustainable change, there won't ever be a *single* solution. Particularly when it comes to the voices in our heads.

I truly believe that everything that is impactful on your business and your mind (because without a strong mindset, you don't have a strong business) comes from working on it over a sustained period of time.

Dealing with the inner critic is no different.

Throughout these pages we will continue to address what the inner critic is saying to you, and why. We'll apply logic to the guff it's spouting by drawing on my experience and the many examples I've collected over the last few years. And we'll look at more helpful and supportive ways we can programme that little voice to enable you to be more in tune with the real you, instead of the "subpersonality" showing up to keep you small.

If you've skipped it, it's essential you go back to the *How to change your mind* chapter now, so you understand the steps to take to unpick the inner critic's stories that we'll continue to identify as we go on.

> **Notice**
>
> **Stay non-judgemental**
>
> **Be kind**
>
> **Apply some logic**
>
> **Neutralise or flip**
>
> **Repeat, repeat, repeat**

Let's recap

1. Let go of the fear of failure and start focusing instead on the journey and the process: who you become through the sheer act of showing up and taking action.

2. Let go of hustle mindset and corporate mentality and truly believe that getting what you want can be fun, easy, enjoyable, and will *not* lead to burn-out.

3. Remember you were born worthy and you deserve and can have everything you desire, just because. No explanation or justification needed.

4. Identify your inner critic, name and characterise it if you find it helpful. Know that they are not you so they stop ruling the roost.

Stop thinking (notice)
Who am I to want more?
Earning well means being burned out
This will never work

Start thinking (flip to)
I was born worthy
I can earn *and* create balance in my life
Things are always working out for me

2

Let's talk about scarcity

Next we need to address one of the most common mindset issues that will hold you back from really making a go of your business. It's something that shows up in virtually every area that you need to tackle if you are to achieve your business goals.

Scarcity (noun)
1. The state of being scarce or in short supply; shortage.[4]

I'm bringing up scarcity now because the natural next step that I take my clients through when setting up their business after goal setting is **niching**. It's the process of getting really clear about the area you want to work in, and more specifically, who you want to help.

As soon as we do this work, scarcity rears its ugly head. 'There's not enough' is a way of thinking that capitalism has brought to bear on us at every turn in modern western-culture life.

I'm absolutely not anti-capitalism. But we do need to remember that the society and economy that we live in thrives when we believe we do not have enough, earn enough, or are not enough, in and of ourselves.

The trouble is, this sense of scarcity rubs off into so many areas of our life and business that it becomes hugely detrimental and holds us back from feeling the opposite: abundant and expansive – which is how we need to feel if we are to really go for it in when building our businesses.

I want to analyse a few of the ways that scarcity has shown up for me as I transitioned into running a business of my own and how I've unpicked them so they haven't scuppered me further down the track.

You think there are a limited number of customers out there

I'm a huge advocate of niching and teach lots of different ways to approach it. But ultimately for me niching is the process of refining *who* you are working to serve.

The more you get to know that ideal customer, the more the content across your website, your social media, your emails, your speaking events, or wherever you show up, can really connect with the person you want to work with.

Let's take me as an example. I have niched down into helping wellness business owners. Whilst my advice, experience and coaching skills could be used to help *anyone* (we were trained in my coaching course that we could coach nuclear physicists if we wanted!), I've chosen to market myself to a particular audience.

That's because a) I *love* these people (people like you) and feel passionate about the work they do. I think it's important and I want to see them succeed. I think the whole world will be a better place if they thrive as business owners.

It's also because b) knowing my niche enables me to create content that speaks directly to my ideal customer. I frequently have people say things such as "what you posted today feels like you're in my head" or "everything you talk about is *exactly* what I'm experiencing!" or "I want to work with you because you *get* me."

That sort of connection, that sort of understanding, is what draws people to want to work with me, rather than any other business mentor. It helps me stand out and be remembered.

However.

As soon as I introduce this concept with clients, scarcity comes up.

> Are there really enough people like this around that I can help?

> Will these people pay for what I'm offering?
> Someone else is serving this group already, are there enough clients to go around?

The answer to all these questions is a resounding **yes**. And the thing is, you *have* to believe that.

Because if you approach your whole business and niche with the thought in the back of your mind "there aren't enough customers that are going to buy this" then that energy, that thought, that doubt, will pervade everything you do.

My client Mary was a classic example of this.

As we worked together to get clearer on Mary's ideal customer, she confessed that what had brought her to work as a Nutritional Therapist was struggling with recurring UTIs (urinary tract infections). Her own experience working with a Nutritional Therapist to make diet and lifestyle changes had seen a total change in her symptoms and inspired her to move into the field and help others.

And yet who were the clients Mary was mostly seeing in her practice? Weight-loss and digestive issue clients.

They weren't fulfilling her and she didn't really *love* working with them. But it was paying the bills and they were coming through the door and she could help them. So she did.

"What's stopping you niching down and specifying you help people with recurring UTIs?" I asked.

"Well it feels a bit too niche. Would there really be enough people wanting help with this?"

Let's apply some logic shall we?

Mary knows she's struggled with this.

Mary also knows that sometimes the clients she sees have UTIs as a symptom.

And looking even generally at the data outside of Mary's own personal experience, Google says that over the last two decades searches for 'UTI treatments' have gone from 20/100 on their interest scale, to 75/100. There are 1.1 million results when you Google 'How do you get rid of UTI without going to the doctor?' People are clearly searching for solutions to this problem.

All the logical evidence points towards the fact this could be a really great, clear niche where there are tens of thousands of potential customers looking for help.

So what's stopping her?

If this is sounding familiar to your own situation and the niche you'd like to go with, please. Hear me when I say, **there are more than enough customers that you want to work with**. For you. For me. *And* for Mary. Way more than you can ever help.

And the critical thing?

They want and need *your* way of doing things.

It may well be that your passion, your 'thing', is something that a lot of other people are doing too.

In our next coaching session, Mary shared that she'd spotted another nutritionist who was specialising in helping people with UTIs. She was basically doing exactly what Mary wanted to be doing, and yet Mary knew this other nutritionist didn't have the personal experience she did.

"It's frustrating because I know I could do a great job really empathising with these people and sharing what I went through and what helped me. But now this other nutritionist has cornered the market, and she's doing really well. I can't niche into this now."

Sound familiar?

You know who you want to help. But there's someone already covering it. Their content seems to be speaking to the same ideal client and, hell, it looks like they're doing an amazing job of it already. They've got a great engaged audience, they're consistent, they're confident, they're getting booked and being chosen to speak at events and all the other things you'd love to be doing.

So where is the space for you?

Right here. Where you are.

Because whilst it might look on the surface like you're doing the 'same' thing, **no one is doing it like you**. And no one ever will.

Because they don't have that magic blend that you do of your experience, your journey, your training, your approach, your way of speaking and explaining.

You. They're not you.

And there is someone out there, many people in fact, that are waking up every morning, despite what feels like a 'saturated market' (to you, incidentally, not them), still struggling with their symptoms and problems.

Whilst I know to Mary it might have felt like there was no room for her to enter this new arena, the truth is that not every person in the world struggling with UTIs was going to resonate and work with this other nutritionist. Or any other nutritionist. They were still struggling. They were looking around. But they weren't finding what they needed.

Because they need *Mary's* way of doing things.

There aren't too many people doing what you're doing. There aren't even a handful of people doing what you're doing.

No one is doing what you're doing. Not like you.

Don't let scarcity win.

You think money is finite and will run out

Money mindset is a whole topic in itself and not something I will cover in full in this book. There are many brilliant people who I recommend you follow and books you can read to improve how you feel about money if it's something you need to go deeper on (and you probably do, we all have money stories).

However, I can't tell you how to build a business, set prices, sell products and programmes, and promote yourself if the way you think about money stinks.

At a basic level most of us emerge into adulthood conforming to the 'it doesn't grow on trees' standard rhetoric when it comes to money. We live our lives with a real feeling of scarcity around money. I know I did.

When I worked in a full-time job in the music industry in London I most definitely lived the entire decade of my life in scarcity. In hindsight, this seems ridiculous because financially it was the most secure I could be, compared to working for myself. Little did I know that though – and wow, I wish I'd worked on my abundance mindset then when I had a regular pay cheque each and every month.

But I didn't. Instead I tracked all of my spending. I had an app that I plugged each and every expenditure into, down to the couple of quid I'd spend on vegetables I picked up for dinner. All that tracking meant I could check a pie chart and assess where all my money was going.

I'm all for tracking your money. It's a good idea. But not when all you focus on is lack.

All that little pie chart showed me, day in and day out, was what I *didn't* have. I tried every week to find ways to spend less money, to keep to a tighter and tighter budget, and I beat myself up when I couldn't save as much as I wanted or spilled over the spending limit I'd wanted to stick to on a night out.

My scarcity mindset made me resent birthdays and weddings and big 'unexpected' costs in my carefully mapped out spending plan. I remember snapping at a friend who sent over the costs for a (perfectly reasonably priced) hen party which I felt I couldn't afford.

I wasn't living and enjoying my money. I was watching it and feeling it was constantly running out. Disappearing.

Instead of looking at what I was earning and the money coming *in*, I was obsessing about what was going *out*.

Does this sound familiar to you?

This type of thinking might have had its use to our

parents when we were kids and they were trying to explain why we couldn't buy yet *another* game or toy that we'd get bored with and abandon within a few minutes. But the problem with it is that it has left us with a worry that money will genuinely run out.

This means when you go to invest in yourself, maybe purchase a much needed piece of training or upgrade your laptop for example, you think the money will be 'gone'. Gone forever. POOF. Disappeared. Never again to return.

Money Coach Ray Dodd explains more about our complicated feelings when it comes to money:

"How you feel about money is not your fault, but it is your responsibility.

We are taught from the day we enter the world that there is not enough for us. This is particularly true for those of us who have traditionally been left out of money making (that is, if we are not white, cis, able-bodied, middle-class men).

Our world is full of societal, cultural and familial stories that there is not enough money out there. And that what money there is, is only available to the select few, the ones who look a certain way, speak a certain way, the ones who work the 'hardest'.

Women, particularly, are conditioned to be carers and nurturers. That is our currency. That is what we have been conditioned to believe we offer the world. Many of us have seen the problems and inequality that money creates. Is it any wonder we find ourselves in a quandary about how to relate to this money stuff when we enter the business world? Is it any wonder we find ourselves attempting to bridge that gap between caring and making money by underpricing and undervaluing our work?

Money is a nuanced topic. For many of us it is not as easy as simply switching our mindset, we have to pay attention to our conditioning too. Unravelling your complicated feelings about money is an important responsibility and it takes time. And that is okay."[5]

Of course, I don't know your situation. It might be that in your life money has genuinely run out before and you've been thrown into incredibly difficult situations and have had to make some really tough decisions. If that's the case, I'm sorry. I am fortunate and privileged enough that this isn't something that's ever happened to me (something we'll look more deeply at in Chapter 7).

But for most of us this hasn't happened.

And even if this has happened to you in the past, it doesn't have to be your reality again.

A coach asked me this right at the beginning of my bid to turn my healthy eating food blog into some sort of business (which is how I wound up being here, writing this book for you): "What's the worst that could happen if you gave it a go?" It's obviously not a hugely optimistic way to look at things on the surface of it. But it is a great question to ask yourself if you're paralysed and too afraid to jump in.

My answer to that question at the time was, "I guess my husband would be able to support me for a little while as I figure things out and start to build up clients. We'd have to cut back on spending for a bit but we could make it work, the mortgage would still be covered. And absolute worst case, if it really didn't work out? I'd just go back to working in the music industry. There are lots of things I can do, I've got lots of contacts."

When I said that all out loud, it suddenly didn't seem so scary any more to give it a go.

Having this conversation is how I turned a repeated negative thought – "I will run out of money" – into a positive affirmation for myself: "I've always had money and I always will."

And this isn't just about you and your money. The urgency to address your 'there's not enough money' thought process is compounded when it starts to ripple out into how we show up and sell what we offer.

If you project your fears and worries about money running out onto your customers and potential clients, it will impact what you charge and how often you ask people to buy – both of which are going to decimate your ability to make this sustainable.

Instead of putting out your services and pricing them at a level that serves both you and them, you will concern yourself with worrying about whether your ideal customers can afford to invest in you and your services if you let scarcity rule. Which will mean a cycle of undercharging, underearning and lack for you. Not a nice place to run a business from.

What your customers can and can't afford is none of your business.

This statement might make you feel uncomfortable. Because you're an altruistic person.

But please know that thinking this doesn't mean you don't care about your customers.

You can still care about people deeply and want to help them, whilst simultaneously being completely removed from the worry about how big their bank account is right now.

This doesn't mean you resort to pushy sales tactics and jumping up your prices just for the sake of it (more on this to come in Chapter 6). And I know you, you wouldn't do this anyway.

What this statement gives you is the ability to stay totally focused on what you do and how you help.

If your ideal customer has a problem, and they believe that problem/ailment/worry/symptom is a big enough issue that they are ready and prepared to address it and get the help they need to overcome it, they will find the money they need to pay for your service.

It is not our job to worry about how much money people have.

I have seen a lot of this worry creeping in particularly, as we live in a post-COVID world. Being around the repeated narrative, whether that's by switching on the news or talking to friends about current affairs, of how the economy is shrinking, people are losing their jobs, their homes and that they're struggling to make ends meet, we assume that *everyone* is in this position and therefore we should lower our prices, offer freebies and discount constantly because *everyone* is suffering and can't afford us.

It's not true. Money hasn't run out. It never has done and it never will do. (Notice how my own affirmation crept in there?)

Whilst some people, of course, struggle in this life, there are many people that have plenty, thank you, and who want and need to invest in what you offer. They're ready. Don't underestimate them or project your money worries onto them. It's none of your business.

Everyone wins when you drop the fear about scarcity around money and start believing there's more than enough to go around.

And if you're a fastidious tracker of every penny like I used to be? Try to look at those numbers and pie charts with gratitude and a feeling of abundance.

When you see your figures, can you write down or speak out loud all the things your money enables you to do, all the goodness you've already received and bene-fitted from as it has gone into and out of your account?

You think there's not enough time to do what you want

Time. This is a massive one. And I have got some short, sharp words to get you back to a logical standing on this form of scarcity mindset. Because if you don't, it's going to *completely* wipe out the prospect of making your business work.

I don't have many fixed 'rules' in the way I help people. But this is one I use in my own life and really want you to take away too because it's a game changer.

We all have the same amount of hours in the day. And whilst I obviously don't know your set-up, your childcare arrangements, your roles and responsibilities, or your day job, I absolutely do know that when you have time to work on your business, there are things you do with your time that are not in your highest interest.

Don't worry. No judgement. We all do it. I'm in the middle of writing this chapter and have picked up my phone and scrolled through Instagram for five minutes rather than getting my words down on the page. No one is immune, definitely not me!

But, as the memes say, "You have the same amount of hours in a day as Beyoncé." And whilst yes, of course, the cynics will retort "yeah but between Beyoncé and her staff, she has more like 3,600–4,800 hours in a day", it wasn't *always* like that for her.

The difference between us and Beyoncé is how she's chosen to *prioritise* her time. How blinkered and focused she's been on the goals she's trying to reach. And how

Let's just agree,
here and now,
that the phrase
"I don't have time"
is banned from
your vocabulary,
never to be
spoken again.

little she lets others and her limiting beliefs distract her and hold her back from using the time she does have, those same 24 hours we all have, to maximum effect.

So please.

Say it with me.

"I do have time."

We all have the same gift of it. It's not about the hours themselves but about what you choose to do with the ones that are available, however few they might be. And if you have a lot of other stuff going on and genuine competing priorities, such as family or taking care of your own health, then be kind to yourself and realistic about what can get done.

Whatever your situation, whether it's loads or very little time you have on your hands, you need to reprogramme the scarcity language you're using right now by replacing "I don't have time" with this new, more challenging but honest, phrase:

'That's not a priority right now.'

"That's not a priority right now" really hits hard. Because if you say "it's not a priority" about things that you actually *know* are your priority, such as getting your website published or pitching yourself to speak at an event, for example, you're holding up the mirror and showing yourself what you're prioritising instead.

It's like me picking up my phone to have (yet another) scroll through Instagram. If I kept saying, "I don't have time to write a book" then I'd never write a book. But if I say, "It's not a priority to write a book", I'd *know* that wasn't the truth. And by picking up my phone mindlessly, I'm just showing myself where my time is really being frittered away.

Your phone is actually quite a handy one to remind you that in fact you *do* have time, because you can now track how long you're on them. Today my phone says I've used it for four hours. FOUR HOURS.

"I don't have time to write a book"? I don't think I have a leg to stand on.

If you don't have loads of time to spend on your business, or even if you do but somehow you end up frittering it away every time you sit down to work on it, I'd advise three things.

1. Use a timer to keep you focused
2. Break things down and work in blocks of time
3. Ask yourself what's the one thing that will most leap you forward

Using a timer to keep you focused

I used to take *so* long writing up my client notes. I would put off doing them and when I got to sitting down to write them 15 minutes would turn into 30, which would turn into 45 or more to get everything together in an email. It wasn't effective or productive.

So I started using a timer. I knew that the notes just needed to be concise and get to my clients in a timely manner. So I set a 15–minute timer on my phone for each set of notes and had it running next to me as I typed. My focus was transformed. It became *so* clear where I would distract myself and wander away from the task in hand. As the timer ticked down next to me, I tightened things up, stopped aiming for perfection and just *got it done*. The timer made such a difference.

Breaking things down and working in blocks of time

Sometimes the thought of doing something big and hairy means we procrastinate, leading us to believe we 'don't have the time'. When really the truth is the task is just *so* large, we can't comprehend getting it done. So our minds default to doing easier, mindless things instead.

When I hear my clients say, "I'm going to get my mailing list set up", I'm inclined to say, "woah there, let's break that down!"

Getting your mailing list set up is a *massive* task. It's got loads of moving parts, lots of new tech to learn and things you'll need to get advice and help on. If you continually write 'Set up mailing list' on your to-do list it's going to be sat there a long time. Your inner critic will turn that monster into a daunting, all-consuming, paralysing task that just never gets done and batters your confidence as it stares back at you incomplete.

I advocate breaking big things like this down into little tasks. For example 'Set up mailing list' becomes:

> Sign up with mailing list provider
> Research a freebie to encourage sign ups
> Design the freebie

> Create a landing page for people to grab a copy of your freebie
> Write an automated email delivering your freebie

Putting each of these into the diary or to-do list, makes it much more likely you'll achieve the overall task of 'setting up your mailing list'.

When I moved all my learning resources over onto a new platform I used this same trick. Rather than writing 'Move everything to new platform' (massive and overwhelming), I wrote a long list of each of the trainings that needed to be transferred and slowly crossed them off one-by-one as I moved them. The sense of satisfaction as I struck them out was pretty awesome as a way to keep me motivated and seeing my progress.

I also fully understand you often don't get long stretches of time to work on things. A lot of people that I help (myself included) have a lot of other things going on that mean getting solid blocks of hours or days to progress things is often impossible.

Beatrice, one of the participants on my group programme, expressed this frustration as she set up her health coaching business while still working full time. She explained to us on one group call how she would be able to get a few things done one weekend, yet it would take her ages when returning to the work again the following weekend to find where she was and get back into the flow of taking action.

Breaking things down into a really clear, easily actionable list of teeny tiny tasks is the antidote to this. It means you'll be able to take action quicker when you *do* get a window in your schedule. You'll be able to say to yourself, "I've got two hours to work on my business this morning, what am I going to get started on?" and immediately be able to pick a smaller, more achievable task to get your teeth into.

And remember, it won't always get finished during that block of time. That's okay (and perfectly normal). You can come back to it later. Every little thing you're doing is all progress. Doing something is better than nothing.

Asking yourself what's the one thing that will most leap you forward

If you are short on time then you want to work on the things that will have the biggest impact. Most clients I work with 1:1 will express this in some shape or form when we start working together: "I want to know what's the best use of my time to get the results I want."

There are loads of things you *could* be doing with your time to set up a business. What you need to prioritise is what will most leap you forward.

Those things for me are:

> Putting together solid offers that will help your ideal customers (you can't make money if you don't have something clear to sell)

> Getting your website sorted (it helps you get found and makes you appear more professional – it's a no-brainer)

> Getting your mailing list set up (you want a way

75

to communicate with people that isn't governed by algorithms and sells for you while you sleep)

> Selling, that is, inviting someone to buy something from you (people don't buy unless you ask them to – more on this and feeling good about it in Chapter 6)

Sometimes these things feel big and uncomfortable. But if you focus on 'what's the one thing that will most leap me forward today?' then it's going to revolutionise how you feel and the results you see in those precious few hours you do have to work on your business.

I hope these little practical tips help you transform your perceived problem with time and the lack of it.

And by the way, if the answer to the question "what is my priority right now, if not this?" is:

> Resting
> Spending time with friends
> Caring for a loved one
> Bringing up children

Then *that's okay*. In fact, that's awesome. They're great, valuable, fulfilling things to do with your hours. They're what makes life worth living and gives purpose and meaning to all the work we do.

But please, acknowledge that's what you're doing with your time. And take ownership of the fact you have mindfully prioritised these things over the work you want to do on your business. Rather than constantly saying "I don't have time."

You don't think you have a big enough audience

Another scarcity mindset I want to explore is one of great significance when you're building a business online – the shortage around the size of your audience.

Now, don't get me wrong. We can't build a sustainable business if we are talking to literally no one. That would be ridiculous.

But what we don't need, contrary to popular belief, is a *huge* audience.

Imagine your favourite cafe filled with 50 people listening to what you have to say. That would feel like a huge audience wouldn't it?

Now imagine your local cinema screening room, every seat filled with 150 people chomping on popcorn and you, stood at the front giving a talk. That would be *massive* wouldn't it?

Go one bigger! Imagine your local concert hall or gig venue. 1,500 people jammed in to see *you* on the stage speaking. That's *a lot* of people, right?!

Try and remember that next time you complain that you don't have 'enough' people following you on social media.

Comparisonitus kicks in. I know it. And we look at others who are seemingly successful who have huge audiences and assume in order to emulate their trajectories, we must accumulate an equivalent following (which feels exhausting and intimidating and usually, in my observations, ends in paralysis).

When I started my blog *The Flourishing Pantry* back in 2016, it was peak wellness influencer time. I stepped onto Instagram in January and started following all the big names. People like Niki Webster from *Rebel Recipes* (289k followers), Jess from *Choosing Chia* (309k followers), Kimberly Espinel from *The Little Plantation* (111k followers) and *Healthy Eating Jo* (168k followers).

It naturally brought out all the comparison. How the hell was I, little-old-me, going to ever get to their level? With my crappy food photos and still working my full-time job, how could I ever do this with my pathetic Instagram audience of a few hundred? They'd all managed to leave their jobs and follow their passion! Did I need to become an Instagram addict to be successful?

I could have thrown in the towel straightaway. Given up the blogging and just looked on enviously at what they were all achieving and believed it was all out of reach. But I didn't.

I chose to flip my mindset. I chose to focus on the people that I *did* have following me (the abundance), rather than the people that I *didn't* (the scarcity and lack).

I looked after those people who were in my world. I talked to them. I took care of them. I replied to their messages. I supported and championed what they did. I celebrated their successes. I met up with them in real life if I could. I checked in on them when they went quiet.

It came back to me tenfold. My community grew. And it gave me everything from which I've built my business.

And yes, before I sign off on this one, I do hear you

saying, "Yeah I get it, Vicky, but my 500 followers on Instagram are not the *right kind* of people that are going to buy from me." We'll talk more about bringing the right kind of people in and what it takes to grow the an ideal following around you (with clever mindset switches, not just marketing tactics!) in Chapters 8 and 10.

For now, trust me when I say – you have a big enough audience to make the money you want. Or the capability to grow one.

Let's recap

1. There are more than enough people that you can help out there. Your way of doing things is needed.

2. There is enough money for everyone. It doesn't run out. It just flows around. Stay focused on helping people with their problems, not worrying about their bank balance.

3. There is enough time, it's just a matter of priorities. What are yours?

4. Your audience is big enough and it's growing all the time. You don't need millions of people watching you in order to make an impact.

Stop thinking (notice)

> There aren't enough people who'll buy this
> I don't have enough money
> I don't have enough time

Start thinking (flip to)

> Clients are everywhere and excited to buy from me
> I have enough money, I always have done and I always will do
> I prioritise my time and use it well

3

Imposter complex and needing to know more

Without a product or service to offer, you don't have a business.

When you put together a package of any kind, whether that's to work with clients one-to-one, offer a group programme, a membership or a one-off webinar or event, it's important to focus on the outcome that you want the customer to have.

People don't buy products. They buy *outcomes*. They buy results. They buy change. They buy what they will be able to think, do, feel, have, know and see after they've spent the time working with you.

When you understand this as a marketing concept you can immediately have more impact in our sales copy and marketing, which means more sales and success.

Rather than getting caught up with all the tangible elements that you could include (such as a workbook, or videos, or recipes, or meal plans, or a long slide-show presentation, or audio guides or whatever it is you think needs putting in there) you should focus instead, when selling, on how the client will feel, think and be after they've worked with you.

Imagine the testimonial that you want to receive from someone going through your offer, and then work backwards to decide what elements need to be included.

In order to be super successful at selling your offer you need to be clear on the outcome that you're offering to potential clients. But it's at this point that some common mindsets may well come up for you.

> I don't know enough to help anyone, I need more qualifications
> What if I put something together and it's not good enough?
> I can't guarantee my clients the changes they want, how will I ever feel confident?

Any of those sound familiar?

It's the final version of scarcity that I wanted us to address and it's a biggie.

So let's break it down and take apart your imposter complex and your desire to know more, rather than **just starting now**.

Why you don't need more qualifications

I'm a big learner. I adore studying and taking in more information. My mum always said she thought I would be some sort of academic researcher or archivist when I grew up. I've always been hungry to absorb information.

But for a long time I completely hid behind this rather than stepping into my own business. I took courses, I read books, I made plans. I did the first and second modules of my coaching training. I watched other people doing well as business coaches and observed the myriad of courses they took – NLP, more advanced coaching certifications, ICF accreditation. I needed these to be like them!

I kept putting another course or programme in the way of me and getting out there. "I'll be ready when I've done that next one."

But it reached a point where I had to stop. I could see that as the months passed that no course, programme or book ever made me feel 'ready'. In fact all they did was upsell me into something *else* I felt I needed, pushing me further and further back.

Eventually I had to make a new year intention for myself to actually *stop learning*. Instead, I resolved to start taking action and getting out there with the skills I already had.

If you are considering taking another qualification in order to put together a package or an offer in this moment I want you to know this.

You are capable of helping people right here and right now, with what you already have in your head.

You are capable of helping people right here and right now, with what you already have in your head.

Read that again.

I can guarantee that however you want to help people, you are more than equipped to do it, in this very moment.

And please, don't get me wrong. I sure as hell don't want any snake oil sellers and dodgy quacks reading this and taking it as licence to sell things they are completely unqualified to offer – I'm assuming they're not my ideal reader and haven't picked up this book.

The sort of person reading this book, the person like you reading these words, is already brilliantly qualified and capable of helping people in amazing ways. Right now.

The sort of person like Helen, one of my clients. When we met, Helen was already more than qualified to help her customers. A Registered Nutritionist and Nutritional Therapist, she'd always taken her CPD seriously. Postgraduate training in Nutrigenomics and an extra course to support people with eating disorders were just a couple of additional studies Helen had undertaken to feel ready to help her clients. But there always seemed to be something more to learn and so a Masters was also well underway by the time we started working together.

The goal for our mentoring time together was to increase Helen's enquiries and bring in more of the ideal customers she loved working with. In order to do this, we got really clear on who that ideal customer was – what they were struggling with and how they'd like things to be without their symptoms.

The clearer we got, and the closer it came to actually doing the marketing and creating the content to attract these customers in, the more Helen's inner critic kept insisting she needed to know *more*.

Firstly, the ideal client – surely it had to be more complicated? Maybe she 'should' be trying to help people with more complex issues? But then that would involve . . . more study and training. Maybe she wasn't ready?

Secondly, something as seemingly simple as posting a blog article triggered in Helen a fear of speaking up and saying the wrong thing. Her inner critic railed against it: it convinced her she didn't know enough to post this simple blog. What if she gave the wrong answer?

Over and over, in a myriad of ways, Helen's inner critic desperately tried to overcomplicate things and tell her that she wasn't good enough to get out there and help people right away. That she need to know more and be more in order to be ready.

When she started to confront and apply logic to these fears, Helen began to realise that doing the Masters wasn't actually about helping more people. It was an attempt to fill the 'not enoughness' that her inner critic was constantly laying on her. In fact she knew that her relaxed, conversational, simple approach actually required little-to-no heavy science to help solve her clients' issues – which meant the Masters was suddenly feeling . . . a bit redundant.

Added to that, Helen started to notice that, far from enjoying the studying, the deadlines and pressure of the

Masters was making her feel stressed. It was taking up her brain space and attention and moving her away from what she actually enjoyed – seeing ideal customers and helping them achieve simple and long-lasting change.

I see this time and time again. It's an inner critic masterstroke.

Brilliantly qualified practitioners. Burdening themselves with more and more and more training in order to feel 'enough' to start helping people. Brilliantly qualified practitioners that feel like imposters.

And the thing about feeling like an imposter?

If you're feeling it, that's a sure fire sign that you're not one.

Real imposters don't feel like imposters.

It doesn't cross their mind for one second that they're scam artists or pulling the wool over people's eyes.

Real imposters have not one ounce of integrity.

They're just going about their imposter business, putting out vacuous offers and not stopping to think about the fact that what they're doing is wrong and is harming, rather than helping people.

Not like you. You have integrity in abundance. Integrity and super high standards of what you are willing to do and put out into the world. You are not a snake oil seller. You are not a dodgy quack.

This is something I learned from listening to a podcast[6] featuring Imposter Complex expert Tanya Geisler:

"You are only experiencing Imposter Complex because you have strong values of integrity, excellence and proficiency in the matters that matter. That's the good news.

The bad news is that it lies to keep us out of action, doubting our capacity, alone and isolated. Those lies tell us we don't belong, we're not ready and so on.

It *does*, however, present with a grain of truth and that truth is: there is room for improvement. There is room for more. So I say that's *also* good news. That means we can always dig a little deeper, reach a little higher, learn a little more . . . again, this is good. Because that means we are deepening our analysis.

Actual imposters? They are deeply unconcerned about integrity and deepening their analysis. The fact that you are experiencing Imposter Complex means you cannot be an imposter. Circular, and Truth."[7]

And let's be clear. This is not me saying you don't ever need to do a CPD course or invest in your own learning ever again. I would strongly advocate for doing both, to continually learn and develop and become the best possible practitioner you can.

But.

The most important thing you'll ever do to improve your craft, make an impact and truly help people is to sell what it is you know about right now. Not to put yourself on another course. Also (affectionately) known as procrasti-learning.

The sliding scale of knowledge

When I first started to realise that I wanted to work for myself, but still didn't have the foggiest what my offer was going to be, I stumbled across the concept of the 'infopreneur':

> An Infopreneur is a person who "starts a business that involves collecting and selling information, especially electronically."[8]

The way an infopreneur is described suggests you don't need to go back to school to become a business owner and have products people will buy.

Instead you can use the knowledge you already have in your head, the things that you feel come naturally and easily and are 'no brainer' information to you and package that up into an offer. Because there are people out there that want that information in your head *and* the way you deliver it.

There are people out there less qualified than you, doing the things that you want to do, simply because they decided to believe in themselves.

Now please, let's take a minute to look at you, dear reader. Because I am really hoping there is a teeny tiny voice inside your head when you're reading this that is saying, "Well . . . I'm definitely one step ahead of that, Vicky. I'm not just an infopreneur. I'm not just peddling any old knowledge in my head. I've learned and studied. I've paid for courses. I do actually know stuff."

There we go.

That's the voice we want to tune into.

Let's put your knowledge on a sliding scale.

This is my favourite visual aid to remind my clients of what they know and are capable of.

The sliding scale of knowledge

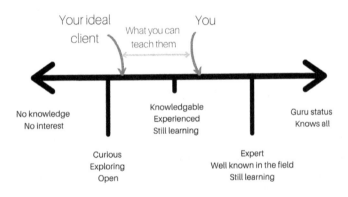

At one end of the scale we have someone who knows absolutely nothing about your area of expertise. They've never even entered your world, heard the words you use or discovered anything about it at all. They're a blank canvas. They are struggling, but they don't have even a drop of what you know to help them.

On the other end of that sliding scale is a guru, a don of your industry. Someone who seemingly knows it all. They've got papers, certificates, masters and PhDs coming out of their ears. Everything there is to know about your subject? They know it. Hell, maybe they even invented some of the concepts you use. They *own* this industry.

There are two important people we need to place on this sliding scale.

You.

And your ideal customer.

Where you sit is a matter of interpretation. More than likely you'll never be the don.

No offence. You're amazing. But the likelihood is you'll never be at the very top of the mastery of your area. And even when we are masterful at our craft, we fully acknowledge that there is always more to learn and the field is always expanding anyway. Nothing is static. No one ever completely stops learning and growing. So that end of the spectrum is always shifting anyway.

The most important point to note on this sliding scale is that your ideal customer is behind you. They might not know absolutely nothing (usually you want them to know a little bit about your field so you don't have to educate them on why what you do is awesome and helpful), but they don't know what you know, with your knowledge and experience.

The distance you are ahead of them might not be a huge amount. But it's a significant enough number of steps that they're looking up this path and wishing they knew the things you know and thought the thoughts you think.

To this end I *do* think the concept of an 'infopreneur' is helpful here.

If you look at your ideal client on that scale and where you are, you can see that you do not need another course or qualification to teach them right now what you know to get the results they want.

I've used the sliding scale of knowledge ms when I've been struck with imposter complex as I've progressed through my business. (It's one that doesn't go away!)

When I started coaching wellness practitioners I didn't have many of the things other similar and more 'successful' coaches had. No six-figure income, no slick set of resources, no accreditation or hours of experience under my belt.

But what I did have was experience of building an online audience, a marketing strategy that I'd learned and adapted that I could pass on, practical know-how about things like website building and using traffic drivers like Pinterest and an ability to get things done that others seemed to lack.

It might not have been much, but it was all stuff that meant I was a few steps ahead of my ideal customers. It was information they wanted. So I started there.

Getting people results – without the complications

As health professionals there is a good deal of snobbery about who helps who and with what. There seems to be an implication that in order to be more worthy, more revered, more respected or in order to get more business, you should be focusing on the complicated cases. The difficult symptoms. The people with a myriad of issues.

I'm here to say, you don't.

Just like my client Helen, you can – and I would argue should – help people with what you *want* to help them with and what comes naturally, easily and effortlessly to you.

If you want to help people with complex cases and that's your bag and you love figuring that stuff out, then all power to you.

I remember listening to a podcast once about a public health official in America who was completely obsessed with investigating the most obscure and unusual tropical diseases that were entering the country.

She traipsed around the States to take samples from corpses and understand more about these weird, wonderful and complicated illnesses, while most of her civil service counterparts stuck to more routine health issues back in their local offices. She became a renowned expert and was consulted widely for her knowledge and expertise in the rare and misdiagnosed.

But for that one official? That was her jam. It's what made her tick. She loved the complicated and obscure.

If that's you. Great.

But you don't have to be a martyr to prove yourself worthy. Remember what we learned in Chapter 1?

You are worthy.
Just the way you are.

You aren't creating a business and serving an audience in order to look like the smartest person in the room (if you are, take a good hard look at what you're doing because your focus is in the wrong place!).

You're creating a business and serving an audience to build an amazing life for yourself *and* have a brilliant impact on the world.

That comes in many shapes and forms. And there are *plenty* of ideal customers that you can help, whatever area it is you want to focus on.

Whatever your version is, it's totally valid.

It doesn't have to be difficult in order to be impactful.

And that goes for your business in general, not just the niche you choose.

One of my first ever clients, Katie, was struggling to make the move from a public sector job to step into her nutrition practice full time. She loved nutrition and her studies and was clearly good at it, judging by the feedback and grades she was getting on her course.

Nutrition was enjoyable. Her 'big job' (as she called it), however, sucked the life out of her. Deadlines, useless colleagues, micro-managing bosses, long hours for little impact. It was hard.

Yet, as we talked about making the move, we identified that Katie had taken on the family belief that work *has* to be hard. "Work isn't something to be enjoyed, it's just a means to an end. It's not something that's meant to be fun" would be the response she'd hear from her parents when she ventured to share her intention to take her nutrition full time. It's tough not to take these statements as facts in the moment, particularly when they come from parents or those we trust.

But 'work has to be hard' is not true. Whilst, of course, many people do not enjoy their work, or maybe you haven't enjoyed your work before now, 'work is hard' doesn't have to be your reality going forward. You get to choose.

Choose what lights you up. Choose what you want to keep waking up and doing, day in and day out. Choose the people you can't wait to help. It can and will work.

But I need to be taken seriously!

I might almost be there convincing you to embrace helping who you love. I might even have begun to help you start to shake off the imposter complex – that feeling that you're not enough – and maybe now you don't feel the need to run off and do another course.

There's another sneaky little mindset that might creep in though that I wanted to WHACK with your permission. It's the little voice that manifests itself in an urgency that many wellness practitioners feel **to be taken seriously.**

> I need to publish research papers for my peers to take me seriously
> I should wear a lab coat and use long science-y words so I get taken seriously
> I shouldn't dance, sing, appear quirky, make jokes or make light of anything around my area of expertise so that I'm taken seriously

◦ Let's put this to bed quickly.

You will be taken seriously when you start seriously helping people.

Read that again.

Being taken seriously is *not* about being someone you aren't, or forcing yourself to do things in your business that don't feel like 'you'. Things that don't bring you joy or play to your strengths.

Being taken seriously comes in many forms. The best way you can be considered a serious player in the area you want to specialise in – and do it consistently and sustainably – is to do what comes naturally to you to help your clients achieve results. You will best achieve this when you stay true to yourself.

• We'll talk more about how to be yourself, get comfortable sharing your story and be visible in Chapter 8. But for now I want to stress that your focus should always be on seriously helping people. With the knowledge you have right now.

Let's talk about being afraid of being busted

I'm terrified of getting busted. A classic trait of imposter complex, I absolutely have the fear that one day someone is going to come along and say, "You realise you actually know *nothing* about what you're doing, don't you? You're a total and utter fraud."

You will be
taken seriously
when you
start seriously
helping
people.

I wanted to write this chapter sharing only stories of how my clients experience imposter complex. I didn't want to share my own insecurities in case as you read the words, you started to feel I'm not good enough to help you.

But my editor caught me: *This chapter needs one of your stories or some short bits that show that you know exactly what your readers are going through. Unless you yourself haven't ever had imposter syndrome . . .?*

Of course I have. And a big part of that imposter feeling for me is the fact that I've never been a health practitioner myself. Which means it's perfectly possible that by putting myself out here proclaiming to know enough to help wellness experts that some people will look at me and think, "You haven't got a clue."

That feels scary of course, particularly if I let my mind linger on it. But I have to accept that's all part of putting myself out here. And harness the visibility and vulnerability of my own imposter feelings, rather than letting them hold me back.

I want to make what might be seen as a weakness part of the story of who I am and what makes me unique and able to help someone like you.

Let's look at the fear of being busted through another story that might also resonate.

Sammy and I worked together one-to-one to help her transition from her corporate job to become a Culinary Medicine Practitioner. We were a great match – Sammy's corporate job was in the arts, as mine had been before I quit, so I could show her the way to build an audience through blogging and social media just like I did.

The plan was that Sammy would finished her qualification and have an audience that knew, liked and trusted her thanks to reading her free content, so they would ready to buy from her straightaway when she graduated.

Simple!

Yet each time we met for our sessions, things weren't moving.

The content ideas and blog post topics we came up with to share her learnings and journey as she studied stalled.

Writing a caption for an Instagram post took forever as she agonised about what she could and couldn't write and whether she'd done enough research. What might people say given she wasn't yet qualified fully? Was she allowed to post? What was in her remit?

Writing a blog post turned from a great idea into an impossibility as her mind went to town. What would people more qualified say? What areas did she feel comfortable to talk about? Sammy was an amazing home cook, she could bake an incredible sourdough and make her own kombucha. How about teaching and talking about those things – no science or qualification needed? Even this felt impossible to own and claim an expertise in.

But there was always the looming question:

"What if I get it wrong?"

It's a classic imposter complex voice that maybe you struggle with too. Your big fear (and Sammy's) is that someone will come along and tear down whatever it is you put out into the world. It might be a social media post, a blog article, a digital product you've created, a seminar or course you want to deliver, you're terrified that someone is going to point out you're 'wrong'.

Here's the thing.

Being in business and, in particular, doing your own marketing, means you are going to be visible. And as a result, you are going to be vulnerable too.

Vulnerable to criticism. Vulnerable to judgement. Vulnerable to opinions.

And so yes, that means there is a possibility, even a tiny one, that someone is going to see what you are sharing and disagree with it.

We need to change how we view this. So that the vulnerability becomes a strength and a sign of growth and progress, rather than something that paralyses you.

Let's give this vulnerability a fresh spin.

Isn't it a good thing that you've put something out into the world that someone can disagree with?

Isn't it amazing that you have made yourself visible enough for others to engage with your content enough to have an opinion on what you're saying?

Isn't this all a sign that your ideal customers are more likely to find you, and recognise that you have something to offer because you're standing out and saying things that help them?

We'll talk more about being 'right' and 'wrong' in the next chapter. But for now, try to reframe what visibility means to you.

Being visible to your inner critic is about being torn to shreds and ridiculed by other practitioners. Or, if you choose to ignore that critical voice, being visible could be about helping people, being your authentic self with opinions and ideas, willing to share, grow and have healthy debate.

* You are not always going to be liked. People are not always going to agree with you.

If you aim in your business to only be liked and agreed with, you will, I'm afraid, blend in and fade out. No one will recognise you and after a while, you'll stop recognising yourself.

I'd obviously love Sammy's story to inspire you because it had a happy ending with her smashing down her fear of being busted by the nutrition police and becoming a super influential Culinary Medicine Practitioner, booking clients left, right and centre and generally bossing her wellness business.

But in fact, things became so stuck that the opposite happened for Sammy – as it does for many people.

Instead of burying herself in more learning, the course that she was meant to be finishing languished. Assignments were left uncompleted. The deadline Sammy had set herself to get the course done came and went without being achieved. And her savings dwindled as she had no clear way to earn as a Practitioner because her qualification wasn't finished.

But what actually happened for Sammy was through starting her blog, sharing on social media and trying to finish her course and imagine herself practising and getting clients, she realised she didn't want to be a Culinary Medicine Practitioner at all.

What she had loved about the whole process was launching her own website. She'd geeked out designing it, learning all the skills to make her site beautiful, easy to navigate and get found online. It was where she really felt in flow and in the zone.

Through this attempt to reinvent herself as a Culinary Medicine Practitioner, she realised that designing websites for other people who shared her passion for the amazing healing power of food, would feel *much* more in line with her strengths. It was something she could really imagine herself doing without fear of judgement or getting it 'wrong'. Blogging about it, talking about it, owning it as her area of expertise? Suddenly *that* felt doable. That felt like her.[9]

So whilst I hope that you will beat this mindset block of fearing the opinions of others, the lesson we can take from Sammy's experience is to give things a go and see who you become on the journey. Stay truly tuned in to what lights you up. Work out what the bits are in this business building journey that make you fizz with excitement and where you lose track of time. Because those are the reasons you're doing this.

But can I get people results?

At the start of this chapter I opened with the knowledge bomb that people don't buy your package or your knowledge, but instead the outcomes and results of working with you.

> They don't buy your one-to-one services: they buy the fact they'll be able to live symptom-free from their endometriosis after working with you

> They don't buy your group programme: they invest so they can finally have a normal relationship with food and get off the yo-yo diet cycle

> They don't buy your video series: they purchase because they're sold on the idea of how strong and clearheaded they'll be now they can finally fit Pilates into their life

It might be that you already knew this. But even if this has come as news to you, you're now realising a whole new doubt is dawning.

What if people don't get the outcome they want from working with me?

What you need to achieve, as a great and confident business owner, is to hold two thoughts simultaneously. Two thoughts that might, to the untrained eye, seem conflicting.

You need to, at the same time, be completely and utterly focused and dedicated on your clients' desired transformation and doing everything you can to help them achieve it AND be completely and utterly relaxed about whether they actually reach said transformation.

This is a tricky blend to accomplish.

In fact you may be reading this thinking, "Vicky, that makes no sense. I'd be a hopeless practitioner if I didn't care about whether my clients get the results they want."

I'm not saying you don't care. You do care. Deeply.

103

I care deeply about whether I get my clients the results they want. If I work with someone one-to-one we spend a good chunk at the start of our first session setting clear goals and objectives for our time together so I can keep us on track.

But they don't always reach them. When we have our final session we revisit the goals. For some, many have not been achieved. (And *hello* to the imposter complex that shows up when I tell you that!)

I could make that mean I'm a failure. That I should pack this in.

But I have to remind myself: my customer's results and outcomes *are not my responsibility*.

Which is why I need to be completely relaxed and release any stress or anxiety I have about whether they reach their goals or not.

What is my responsibility?

How I show up. The quality of the work I do with them in our time together. The commitment I give.

Whether they do or don't get the outcomes they want from our work together is not something I can control. All I can control is what *I* do in the relationship. I have to allow them the gift of their own transformation.

I don't dictate what happens. I am only one side of the exchange.

This is exactly the same as goal setting. We can set goals like signing five new clients this month, hitting 1,000 followers on Instagram or earning €5,000 in your business.

But technically none of those things are in your control. All these goals require *other people* to take an action. All we can control is what *we* do to make those outcomes happen.

It's also exactly the same as we are taught in the self-development world. Those people who are the most depressed, the most anxious and the most chronically stressed in society are those who try to control other people and the world around them.

As a result, these are the people among us that are relentlessly disappointed and let down by the rest of the world when it doesn't live up to expectations or conform to the plans they had in mind. It's an endlessly depressing way to live out your existence on this planet, because controlling other people is not how we work as sociable human beings or how we make the most of this one, precious life we're given.

And it's funny because I bet as you read this, as someone who I'm sure has done the self-development work and knows to let go of trying to control your kids, your partner, your boss, your mum or whoever it is that has caused you anxiety in the past, you'll only now be realising that the same principle applies here too.

That same release of control can be used here, to how we think about and treat our customers.

You are not in control of your client's actions or outcomes. You are only in control of what *you* bring to the party.

If we don't get this right we can become extremely wound up, anxious and obsessed about our clients and customers. And I don't mean in a healthy way.

You have to release. Let go. And know that you have

brought all of your tools and applied all of your attention and focus to help get your client the outcome they want. And that is the best you can do.

Keep learning – but live in the now

One of the key messages of healthy living is the importance of living in the present. A surefire way to help with everything from anxiety to overeating, being in the moment is the answer to many of the modern day wellness issues you as a practitioner help tackle.

Feeling anxious? Take a deep breath and check in with the body. Notice your toes, your fingers, your jaw, the tension in your forehead. Being in the moment, the anxiety eases.

Overeating? Eat your food mindfully; smelling, tasting, chewing and enjoying every sensation of taking a bite, rather than eating while distracted. Being in the moment, the overeating stops.

Let's apply that same brilliant, wellness logic to your compulsion to keep learning.

Feeling like you don't know enough to help people right now? Take a deep breath and check in with the body. Be in this moment, right here and right now. Remind yourself of all the training you've done to this point, the experience that got you here, the people who already admire you and ask for your help and advice.

You will always learn more. You'll always be growing as a person and a practitioner. Nothing will stop that.

But what you need to do in order to step into the brilliant business owner you are, is live in the moment, with the skills and expertise you already have.

All we have is right now. We are never 'there'. We're never 'done' with training. We've never learned *everything*. There is always something new to add to our tools.

But the only time we live in is the present. So this is the moment you need to take action and start showing up for the people that need you. Those people that are a few steps behind you, that need and want *your* way of helping.

When you're worried your magic is fading

It might be that you're reading this book having recently graduated or perhaps you are close to finishing your course or degree. All your learnings and studies are fresh in your mind. You've worked closely with lecturers, peer groups, received gradings for your work in the last few weeks and months and done observed coaching sessions or practice clinics with guinea pig clients. It's all feeling recent and tangible and you can still reach for your textbooks now if you need to check on something quickly. You're feeling pretty confident in your ability to help people.

That's a great place to be in. What I'd love for*f* you to capture is the confidence you're feeling in this moment in your newfound learnings and understandings. Because, and this is a tough one to swallow, you're going to need to channel that confidence over the next few weeks and months as your attention turns to building a *business*, instead of building your skills as a practitioner.

There will be a period of time, inevitably in your first year and for some of us longer, when you're not using the skills you trained in on a regular basis. Instead you'll be trying to get your head around marketing techniques, copywriting, website building and sales skills, not to mention trying to figure out your finances and tax. And just generally working your arse off to bring in customers.

This can create a slow, creeping doubt that if you did actually get a paying client . . . would you remember how to help them? Could you *actually* get them the results they're looking for? Would you get on a call and totally fall apart and not remember the first thing you were meant to say?

Make sure that as you tackle and immerse yourself in the business building part of your journey that you find ways to keep reconnecting with your practice.

And no, I don't mean sign up for a gigantic additional training course! I mean reading books, listening to podcasts, chatting to other practitioners, thinking about ways you can run through your skills and training and procedures. So that you feel 100% prepared for that amazing moment when someone gets in touch and says, "I need your help, can we talk?"

Let's recap

1. You don't need more qualifications. Remember the sliding scale of knowledge – you know more than the people who want your help. You can always learn more, but you are already ahead of them and can impart wisdom.

2. Your work doesn't need to be complicated in order for you to be highly regarded and well recognised. Keep it simple and true to yourself and what you love doing.

3. You cannot control your clients' outcomes and results. All you can control is your own hard work and dedication to their journey. Let it go.

4. Live in the present with the amazing skills and knowledge you have. That's all we get. We only run our businesses from the here and now, not from an imagined future where we know it all.

5. If you're worried your skills as a practitioner are fading over time if they're not being used regularly, find ways to reconnect and remind yourself so you feel totally ready and excited that someone is about to book in.

Stop thinking (notice)

> I don't know enough
> I should be doing something more complicated
> I can't get people results

Start thinking (flip to)

> My clients need me and what I know
> I am learning more every day that enables me to help people
> I have all the tools my clients need to get results

4

Making the right decision

As you lay the foundations for your business you'll start to create products – maybe a fabulous one-to-one programme or workshop. They will include all the structure, tools and resources you know will totally transform and change your clients' health.

And privately, at your computer in the comfort of your own home, you'll be feeling a bubble of excitement and pride at what you have put together and how many people it has the power to help.

And then . . .

There it will be.

The thought that will sabotage you and stop you getting this amazing offer out into the world.

What if this is the wrong offer?

This is one that's going to come up a lot.

What's the *right* thing to do?

What's the *right* choice here?

What if I get it *wrong*?

The worry about getting it right or wrong will paralyse you if you don't let go of thinking this way.

I'm going to let you in on one of my favourite coaching tools:

What if I told you there was no 'right' or 'wrong' decision?

It's not a trick.

It's the truth.

Rather than agonising over every option and choice as you build your business, know that there *is* no right or wrong decision. At any stage in your journey. I do not care at all what any business guru has told you.

There is just a decision. And then a series of actions and consequences that will take place as a result of you making that decision.

Honestly. You can't get it wrong.

You cannot make the wrong decision.

Liberating, isn't it?

How to reframe your 'mistakes'

But you might be thinking, "I get it, Vicky. There's no such thing as 'wrong'. But when I look back at what's

112

You cannot make the wrong decision.

happened in the past and some of the things I decided to do, they sure as hell feel like they were the wrong decisions."

And I relate hard to that.

Those decisions that make your toes curl thinking about them. That make you cringe as you relive them over and over in your mind.

I've got those too. I'm not immune.

When I was in the early days of trying to figure out how to make my healthy eating blog into a money maker, I launched an online course. The darling child of the online world. An instant win, passive income generator, it seemed like the logical thing to do.

I was going to put together a pre-recorded course all about how to stack your cupboards for healthy eating. Sell it. And make loads of money.

Great decision, right?

Wrong. Or at least, it felt wrong.

Because the course was a total disaster. I didn't make a single sale.

And that was despite spending hours filming and editing the content, paying for a platform to host the course, buying a domain name and promoting the course through Instagram, Facebook and to my email list.

On reflection it was clear why it was a total flop: I did zero market research, I had no belief in the transformational properties of the course, I was *terrified* of asking for money from people (hello money mindset blocks! More of this in Chapter 6) and I totally hid from the marketing process.

It would be very easy to look back on this as totally and utterly the *wrong* decision to have made in the early days of my business.

And yet I don't.

What I've come to learn is when we take a decision in our business, we get to choose how to think about the outcome.

Our mind's default position (and our inner critic's happy place) is to point out that bad or negative outcomes from our actions are signs that:

> I'm failing
> I'm useless
> This will never work
> Stop trying, stay safe

These are the thought patterns that we've lived with and had ingrained in us for years. Launching a total flop of an online course as my first-ever attempt to make money from my passion project side hustle, I could have made it mean all these things.

But when running our own business, we need to realise these thoughts are exactly that: just thoughts.

They aren't reality.

They aren't facts.

They're statements that our brain has made up.

And why has your inner critic made these up in the face of negative things happening?

Because, as we've said, it's trying to keep us safe.

That's literally it's job. To keep you from doing

115

things out of your comfort zone. Stay safe. Keep doing the same things. Don't rock the boat. Don't do anything that might put you at 'risk'. Stay alive, at a basic primal level.

It's time to show that inner critical voice some kindness (remember that's step three in *how to change your mindset*, go back and remind yourself if you need to do so). It got you this far and you're still here, alive and functioning in the world. That's a good thing!

But if we're going to drive forward and do hard things, we need to reframe what we think is going 'wrong'.

When we don't make a single sale on our online course, when we don't convert a discovery call, when we post to social media and get tumbleweed, when we write ten pitches to corporates and get no responses. Whatever those signs are that we're doing it 'wrong'. Instead of assuming the worst, we need to think:

> Doing this proves I'm out of my comfort zone
> I've learned something from giving this a go
> Taking this action moved me further forward than doing nothing
> I'm actually pretty awesome to have even tried this
> I'm lapping everyone on the sofa (This is one of my favourites. My sister said it to me when I was marathon training, and I think is perfectly applicable to business too!)

Thinking like this is *way* more likely to encourage and motivate you to keep showing up, as opposed to reading the signs that you're doomed and it's not working. I choose to think about my disastrous first attempt at an online course as follows:

1. I learned loads about video editing which will come in use for something else.
2. I tested out a learning platform where I could sell courses in future and know how to set it up quickly and easily next time.
3. I had some interesting conversations with people about what I'm trying to sell that taught me what people are and aren't interested in.
4. I realised that selling content around cooking and healthy eating just really doesn't fill me with joy but makes me shrink instead.

Taking this empowered approach to what might have appeared like a 'wrong' or 'bad' decision helped me to dust myself off and keep going – to the place where I am here today, writing a book for you.

You are the scientist in a great big experiment

One of the first coaches I worked with, Kerry Lyons, taught me an invaluable way to look at my business when I was just starting out. It was a fundamental lesson that one of her own mentors introduced her to and it really helped me to build on this idea of reframing decisions and steps we choose to take in our businesses that might not work out or be profitable – it might be a metaphor that you find useful too.

Whenever I am contemplating launching something new (because yes, I kept trying to sell things, even after that first disaster!), upping my prices or trying something different and getting all the wobbles and worries, Kerry would say to me:

"See it all as an experiment. Imagine yourself like a scientist. You've got your goggles on, your white lab coat, your gloves. You're in front of a table covered with test tubes and flasks filled with liquids and potions.

And you're experimenting. You're adding a bit of this and a dash of that. You're trying things out.

And then when you're done, you step back and assess the results. What worked? What didn't? What could you do more of? What would you do less of next time?"[10]

It's all one big experiment.

When you approach business decisions with this scientific approach, you become a lot less obsessed with getting things 'right' or 'wrong'. You simply take action in order to get data. Feedback and information on what to do next.

It's not a case of doing something in your business, for example, launching a course, and then it either being a huge success or a massive failure. Instead, it's about *doing something*, for example, launching a course, and then *learning from the process*. How did I market it? What worked? Who came? What price did I set? What questions did I get asked? Was the platform I used any good? How can I improve next time?

In his book *Think Again*[11], Adam Grant argues that harnessing the methods scientists use helps us to reduce the influence of our own personal feelings or opinions on the actions we choose to take. Considering many of you reading this book will be well informed, science- and evidence-backed practitioners who love a dive into the latest research, I feel I'm talking to like-minded people when I stress the importance of a scientific approach not only to your practice, but also to your business.

Rather than treating our beliefs as truths, Grant encourages us to treat them as hunches instead.

Hunches can be tested, as scientists test their hypotheses. Taking this scientific approach to difficult problems or decisions we must make often yields better results in politics, life *and* business.

What if your 'hunch' is that it's a great idea to launch a course?

You test it. And then you stand back and assess your learnings in order to improve and get better results next time.

It's simple science.

Nothing is ever a waste of your time in business

Maybe I've got you on board a bit more about 'mistakes' and experimenting in your business.

But to go back to the whack-a-mole analogy, another way this worry about getting it 'right' rears its ugly head is feeling like some things you choose to do are a *waste* of time.

I genuinely believe nothing you ever do in your business is a waste of time. And personally, I include those things such as:

> Hours spent working out how to automate your mailing list
> Writing sales pages for events you never even promote
> Creating content for a course that doesn't sell a single place

I have done all these things.

I truly believe that doing these things, and many more, that some may consider a 'waste of time', have taught me valuable lessons.

They've made me faster in the long run. They've given me skills I didn't have before. They've helped me hone my craft and offer and create something I can repurpose and use elsewhere. They've helped me to have better conversations and built great relationships.

Nothing is a waste to me. It all adds up.

And okay, I do get it. Some things feel like a waste if you are genuinely not good at them, or (more importantly) have any inclination to become good at them.

I do talk to my clients a lot about staying in their 'zone of genius', a phrase made famous by Gay Hendricks in his book *The Big Leap*[12] to describe the things you are uniquely good at and love to do. And whilst I'm a massive (massive!) proponent of doing things yourself, you can (and should!) of course outsource some aspects of running a business whenever you are able to if they're not enabling you to do your best work.

You can't possibly be good at everything and there simply aren't the hours in the day for you to be the administrator, accountant, marketing manager *and* practitioner in your business.

But if you are in the early stages of starting your business, when it's just you and next-to-no money to invest in help, see everything you spend your time on as valuable.

Flip that mindset.

Delete the phrase, "this is a waste of time" from your vocabulary.

Insert "everything I do is all adding up to the business I desire".

The worry about getting it wrong in the world of health advice

I work specifically with health and wellness practitioners. This is made up of people trained in professions such as Nutritionists, Nutritional Therapists, Health Coaches and Personal Trainers.

I am not a health practitioner. I've never trained to give out health advice of any sort. But I have, to my shame, been a rather reckless health blogger in my time.

When I first started out trying to improve my own health and making changes to my diet and lifestyle to tackle IBS symptoms, I thought it was acceptable to simply post on my blog my thoughts, a few cobbled together suggestions and bits of research I'd found on the first page of Google to support my theories.

Obviously not clever.

The more I learned and immersed myself in the world of health, the more I realised the sense of responsibility we all need to have working in this sphere. I understood as I expanded my network and knowledge that each practitioner has a place and a qualification level and is uniquely placed to give specific advice, support, and diagnosis.

As a blogger with absolutely zero qualifications (nor any inclination to go back to school to study the science) my place was right at the bottom of the scale for advice. All I could do was share my experiences, learnings and recipes to inspire people, but give absolutely *no* advice or "eat like me – get results like me!" type content.

I learned, slowly but surely, to stay in my own lane and leave the advice to the professional health experts. And, as it happens, through writing that blog I swiftly discovered the stuff I actually liked helping people with wasn't how to stock their cupboards for healthy eating and cook nutritious food. It was all the marketing, mindset and business stuff that people were asking me for! Hence being here today writing *this* book, instead of a cookbook.

I digress . . .

What I'm trying to say is that *you* may well be one of these real experts. Someone who has studied, practised, submitted assignments, completed assessments, and passed exams to allow you to give health advice to others.

And I know, from having worked with hundreds of you now, that there *is* a level of responsibility that comes with what you do.

Technically speaking you *could* get it 'wrong'. You could give bad advice. You could affect someone's health negatively rather than positively with your recommendations. You could even get sued. It happens.

Even if you don't feel worried about this right now, it can also sneak up on you. Rebecca, a client I worked with one-to-one for a Power Hour, said that over the years she had been practising as a Nutritional Therapist, the voice of her inner critic had started to get louder and louder, instead of quieter and quieter.

Slowly but surely, as Rebecca helped more and more people, she started to hear that inner voice of doubt increasing in volume. It was saying things such as, "You're going to get caught" or "Something bad's going to happen." At its peak, it would lash out with, "You're going to kill someone one day!"

That's a horrific mindset backdrop for trying to motivate yourself to show up and get clients.

I don't want you to feel like that.

This phenomena of becoming more, rather than less, worried about getting it 'wrong' as you progress exemplifies the classic Dunning Kruger Effect and is precisely what I discovered on my health blogging journey too.

It goes like this.

At the start: Wow this is amazing, let me tell you all about this stuff I know!

A couple of months in: Oh wow . . . this is so much more complicated than I thought it was . . .

A few months later: There is so much to learn I will *never* fully understand this (otherwise known as the valley of despair).

A couple of years on: It's starting to make sense now the more I've learned.

Five years or so after you began: Trust me, it's complicated!

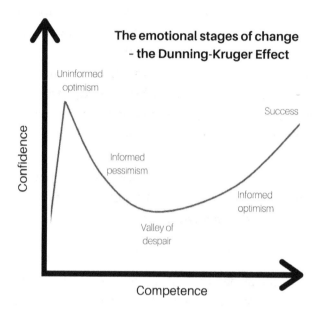

The emotional stages of change
- the Dunning-Kruger Effect

Uninformed optimism

Success

Confidence

Informed pessimism

Informed optimism

Valley of despair

Competence

There will be a point, if you're someone who really values science, research and evidence (and I know this is most of you who are reading this), that you realise there is so much nuance and so much to know that you will never ever be the guru you once thought you might become in your field of health.

Being at the 'I will never fully understand this' point is terrifying. And I've seen it become totally paralysing when it comes to taking action to grow your business.

I am not a legal expert, so I can't advise on contracts or legalities. But the woman who is the expert that I trust with the legally binding aspects of my own work (and, whilst a lawyer now, was a Personal Trainer in a former life) is Lucy Wheeler, also known as Lucy Legal. (See, I'm staying in my own lane here and getting the expert in. I've learned my lesson!)

Lucy and I share a passion for ensuring you and all your amazing knowledge is being used, rather than allowing the fear of getting it wrong paralyse you into never helping a single soul. Because that would be a crying shame.

From an expert's point of view, here's what Lucy recommends to keep getting it 'right' when it comes to professional health advice:

"The fear of getting things wrong in business is a valid one. For most, getting it wrong means you'll get a complaint and possibly a refund request. For some it means you'll face legal action. But for those in the health industry the scope of getting it wrong could create a serious negative impact on someone's life. Whilst that might sound scary, the good news is that the legal elements of running a business are a lot more straightforward than people think.

The first thing you must do is ensure that you are qualified in your specialist area and then, crucially, that you stick to that area of expertise. Whilst you may worry that this will limit your earning potential it actually has the opposite effect. I work with a range of entre-preneurs and it is those who are specialist who are the most sought after.

Once you're qualified with a reputable body it becomes much easier to put effective insurance cover in place and to begin the process of protecting your business with contracts, policies and trademarks.

Having a contract in place does more than just prevent you from getting sued. It helps you to protect your business, create boundaries and clearly communicate your responsibilities and what you'll be delivering as part of your offering."[13]

Beyond Lucy's recommendations here, whilst of course there is always a possibility that things *can* go wrong, you must remember that only a very small minority of practitioners get sued or into trouble in their practice.

It might look like 'lots' of people experience this from the online forums you're in sometimes. It might feel like a very realistic possibility because the scale of the problem has been blown out of all proportion by your inner critic. Or perhaps you read a horrific story in the press.

But it's not true. Being sued and getting it horrendously wrong is *not* the norm. It does not have to be part of your experience as a business owner.

The Law of Attraction[14] is the belief that the universe creates and provides for you what you focus your thoughts on. Whether you subscribe to it wholeheartedly or think the whole thing is pseudoscience, there is a bit of evidence that it hangs on that we could tap into here.

The more you focus on something, the more you see of it.

It's called the Baader-Meinhof effect.[15] When your awareness of something increases, it leads you to believe it's happening more, even if that's not really the case.

If you spend every hour of the day allowing your mind to continually keep revisiting the thought that you might get sued and get it wrong, then you're going to keep seeing more evidence that it will happen. I'm not going to say thinking this way will *make* something bad happen, that's ridiculous. But the focus and attention you keep giving it will mean your mind keeps seeking out evidence to reinforce your belief.

You will see the bad news in the press. You will zoom in on the tales of woe top of your newsfeed. Your fears will be the talk of the town when you chat to your college peers.

If, however, instead you take the practical steps I've outlined above to protect yourself and then focus your time and energy on marketing yourself to dream clients, growing your skills and doing your work, whilst cultivating an "I am safe to practise and help people" mindset, you're going to see a lot less of the scary 'prosecute' culture. Look at all the good that can come from you practising. The clients you'll help, the impact you'll have, the people you'll meet, the places you'll go, the freedom it will allow, the creativity it will release, the benefits to your family and friends.

Changing your mindset won't completely insulate you from ever being sued. But it can help you show up, keep positive and attract the right kinds of people who are less likely to give you problems down the line. Your energy will be drawing those people in who get and value you. Rather than the ones who want to pick a fight.

The briefest of words on perfectionism

I can't finish this chapter on getting it 'right' without touching on perfectionism. Experimenting and letting go of 'right' or 'wrong' is a real stretch for many of the people I work with who profess to be current sufferers of or in recovery from the stranglehold of perfectionism.

You'll identify as a perfectionist if:

> You set impossibly high standards for yourself and beat yourself up when you don't reach them
> You won't launch or release anything until it's absolutely perfect – you draft and sit on things because there's always more tweaking to be done
> You're sure someone will point out your mistakes and errors if you put out anything subpar so it's better not to put it out at all

Perfectionism is just another clever, whack-a-mole mindset way of your inner critic telling you you're not good enough. And if it's a mindset, it's something we can work with and change in order to grow into thought processes that are more helpful and empowering.

Let's apply some logic, shall we?

Nothing, ever, in any walk of life, least of all your new fledgling business, is going to be perfect.

Reid Hoffman, founder of LinkedIn is often quoted as saying, "If you are not embarrassed by the first version of your product, you've launched too late."[16]

If you're a perfectionist or have perfectionist tendencies this might be a difficult one to embrace. But it's one I've wholeheartedly jumped on board with as I've grown my business to stop me dithering and nit-picking over what I want to put out into the world.

Accepting that what I put out now will almost inevitably embarrass me in a few years' time means I'm at peace with just getting on and doing it. Posting that blog. Launching that product. Sharing those photos. Sending that pitch.

Fussing more won't ever help me reach perfection any way. Getting to a place that I'm happy enough with it, that I've given it my best shot, and that I can stand by the process and intention behind it, means it's ready to be out there. Time to hit 'publish'.

Now I just need to stop fussing and rearranging full stops and paragraph breaks in this chapter and accept that this is the best it can be right now in order to hit 'publish' and give you the recap . . .

Let's recap

1. There is no such thing as a 'right' or 'wrong' decision in your business. There's just a decision and a series of actions and consequences. Stop worrying you're going to get it 'wrong'. You can't.

2. Reframe how you see mistakes or things not working out. Rather than seeing them as signs you're failing or not cut out for business, see them as evidence that you've pushed out yourself of your comfort zone and are growing.

3. Imagine yourself as a scientist in everything you do in your business. See everything you choose to do as an experiment that gives you evidence to go forward. Keep filling those test tubes and adjusting your potion.

4. Nothing is ever a waste of time in business. Even if a task feels relentless and your brain is screaming that you're rubbish at it, I promise it all adds up to skills and knowledge that will serve you in the future. It all teaches you something.

5. Things can go 'wrong' if you help people with their health. Protect yourself as much as possible and

focus on the positive possible outcomes of doing your work, rather than the negative.

Stop thinking (notice)
> I'm going to do it wrong
> I'm a failure, it didn't work out
> I'm going to get sued
> It has to be perfect

Start thinking (flip to)
> I learn from everything I try
> Everything I do in my business is taking me one step closer to my goals
> I attract clients that I can help easily

5

Finding your own path

What I want to pause for in this chapter is a deeper dive into business models and how your amazing knowledge and expertise can make you a sustainable income.

I'm not talking a flash-in-the-pan, one-off launch that leaves you exhausted and then wondering where the next client will come from. I'm talking about building consistent income streams and audiences that keep trickling into your inbox and bank account each and every month, so your business truly serves you as well as your customers.

Sounds good right?

How do we do that?

The beauty (and, sometimes, the difficulty) with creating your own business is that you can make money in *many* ways.

I don't care what any other business guru has told you: there isn't a single fixed, guaranteed way to make income.

A client of mine, let's call her Josie, once came to me to say she'd listened to some business advice online from another coach in which it was claimed, "Everyone *should* have a product in their offering that's a £3K 6-month programme with payment plans." Josie came to our next session asking if I agreed and what should her £3K, 6-month offer look like?

My answer?

No, I don't agree.

I don't believe there are *any* shoulds in business.

Should, generally, is a pretty negative word in life, and definitely a negative word when growing your own income streams. Because with 'should' we suddenly feel pressured and obligated to do business in a particular way that doesn't feel aligned with our preferences or values. (The latter we'll be going into in more detail in Chapter 6.)

The reason that there isn't a one-size-fits-all business model is because we're all different.

The only thing you *should* do in your business is what's right for *you*.

We all have different strengths. We all feel called to serve and do our work in different ways and we all light up and feel energised by different formats.

The only thing you *should* do in your business is what's right for you.

> Your business could be purely one-to-one client work. A small number paying a higher price to get the most personalised, bespoke service you can offer them.

> Your business could be purely courses and group programmes. Larger groups paying lower prices to get information and support inside a container.

> Your business could be all digital pre-recorded products and content. No need for you to be present at fixed times, your suite of offers is available anytime.

> Your business could be a blend of all three of these; a particular balance and ratio that suits you and serves your clients in the best way you know how.

Remember what we said in the last chapter? There is no 'right' or 'wrong' way to do this. There is a just a decision about your business model – using the information and knowledge you have at this moment in time – and then a series of actions and consequences that will come from that decision.

That being said (and I promise I'm not about to completely contradict myself!), what you can't do is make a good, sustainable income by charging a very small amount to a very small number of people.

Small audience + small-priced products does not = great business.

If you genuinely believe that all that amazing knowledge and information in your head can become your breadwinner – and want that – then you need to apply *some* strategy to what you sell and the price to ensure it does.

Remember we talked about scarcity mindset back in Chapter 2? This is where we need to make sure it's not creeping in.

It can feel natural when we reach this stage in the process and start putting together products to think small. To think low numbers, low prices and what feels comfortable and 'achievable' to sell right now.

If you start off like this, you're setting yourself up for a fall.

And no, I'm not about to say you should start off with a million-dollar programme – that's not my advice to anyone at the beginning of a business-building journey.

But don't assume the first thing to do is go super low.

It's time to put on the blinkers

I once did a Q&A session for a well-known nutrition college. One student, let's call her Maria, shared the situation she had found herself in when it came to the products she was offering, a situation which is all too common when I talk to recent graduates.

"I've been working on my business for over a year now," Maria said. "Social media is hard work, creating content, being consistent, putting out blogs. I'm exhausted. I've put so much time into it, but it's getting to the point where I'm starting to wonder if it's worth it."

"What is it you've been selling?" I asked.

"I created a really affordable online course that people can buy from my website. It's only £30. It took me ages to put together and it's packed with information. But I haven't sold a single one. If people won't even buy something cheap, how will I ever make this into a real income?"

Sound familiar?

This is where my business models question needed to come in.

"What's your business model? What made you choose a low-priced course to start off with?" I asked.

Maria replied, "Well, I had a look around at what other people were doing who are in a similar field to me and that's what they seemed to be offering. I thought I'd do the same."

Right.

Can you see the problem here?

There's a reason that many online business coaches talk up starting out with 'high ticket offers'. That is because if you're going to put in *all* that effort into marketing yourself, building up an audience, spending hours on social media, sending content to a mailing list, speaking and writing and guesting for others to grow your reputation (some of which Maria clearly had done), it's 'easier' at the end of that to sell a higher-priced offer to one or two people than it is to sell to a lower-priced offer to one or two hundred.

If you spent a year growing your audience and brand and then only made ten sales of your £30 course, that's not going to feel like a great investment of your time, is it?

On the other hand, if you spent a year growing your audience and brand and then made ten sales of your £3,000 bespoke one-to-one service, that's suddenly looking a lot better for your bank manager.

I put 'easier' in inverted commas. Because getting ten people to pay you £jodie,000 each is not simple or easy if you've never done it before. And it does involve you having the right approach and the right beliefs.

I hope with that very simple maths equation you can see that choosing to launch a cheap course, simply because it looks like what other people do, and plays to your scarcity mindset of what people will be willing to pay, isn't the best place to start.

Here's the problem with creating your business based on what you think others are doing.

You do not know the full story of someone else's business.

If, like Maria, all you can see is a cheap product on a peer's website, what you don't know is:

> Whether this is a cheap product that then leads into higher-priced offers that are upsold afterwards (perhaps not listed on their website)
> Whether they're totally loaded or bank rolled by a wealthy partner or inheritance that means they don't really care about making an income
> Whether they've sold any of these products at all
> Whether they have a clue what they're doing from a business perspective

And I don't say all that to put down your peers and others out in the market. Many will be doing a fabulous job and be making great money.

But they're not you. The only person whose business you know everything about, be it finances, preferences and strengths, is **you**.

It's time to put the blinkers on.

Rather than picking your business model based on what other people are doing, you need to step back and tune back in to where we started with Chapter 1. With *your* goals and *your* vision.

You need to truly believe that there are infinite ways to build a sustainable income and that the way that feels right for you *can* and *will* work if you put the right energy and time into it.

What business models are there?

If you're a complete newbie, just as I was when I started to run my coaching business, it's totally normal to not have a clue what to offer or where to start. It's all well and good being told you can do 'anything', but I know you. You'd like to follow even a rough plan of what is likely to work rather than flinging spaghetti at the wall, am I right?

So I wanted to simplify the business models I see working well in the wellness and online business world and share with you four distinct archetypes for making money.

As I've already said though, this doesn't mean there are *only four ways to make money*. You can still take bits from these or adapt and create your own model and still be successful.

However, if you're starting with a totally blank slate and no experience at all, you might like to think which of these models appeals to you most when it comes to designing a business that lights you up.

Influencer Izzie

> Designed around creating a personal brand and reputation, primarily based in large amounts of free content creation. This content is shared on a website/blog, social media, a YouTube channel or podcast.
> Relies on the consistency and volume of your free content to create a large loyal audience that know, like and trust you, of which many will buy from you if you offer the right thing.
> Income is earned by selling access-anytime products or a select number of one-off webinars on your chosen topic.
> Income also comes from brand partnerships and advising and/or corporate work, both more easily attracted because of your high profile.

Pros

> Opportunities will land in your lap if you create a brand around yourself and what you do. You'll be invited to do things, such as write a book, speak for businesses who like your high profile, be a guest on podcasts, and so on.

> A flexible lifestyle, with a business based around anytime access products or a select number of speaking or one-off time specific events that you dictate.

Cons

> You will need to be consistent in creating content on a long-term basis, even when for an initial period this won't result in income. You need to create a big loyal audience which takes time. Initially you might need to do this alongside another way of earning income (a full or part-time job for example) while you build your brand.

> High profile isn't for everyone, as well as lots of lovely opportunities, your visibility means there is more of a chance of being criticised.

CASE STUDY: CHARLOTTE STIRLING-REED (SR NUTRITION)

I came across Charlotte and her work when I was still health food blogging when I was invited to a press event for a dairy brand launching a new high fibre product. Charlotte was the resident nutritionist with the brand, present on the day to answer questions posed by the bloggers and add the science and stats behind the product.

Charlotte began her working life in the NHS after gaining a degree in Nutrition and Human Biology and then a Postgraduate Degree in Nutrition and Public Health. Since then, Charlotte has worked in various areas but has clearly niched into her specialist area – baby nutrition – and used her social media to grow a following and brand for herself in this area.

Starting her Instagram account at the end of 2014, Charlotte has built her reputation by creating free resources on her account and her website, to help her audience at each stage of their child's feeding journey. This consistent release of informative, specialised content has led to her working with Joe Wicks on his book *Wean In 15*, brand features and collaborations with big name baby goods suppliers such as Stokke, Aveeno and Ergo Baby Carriers, and her own book deal from the Ebury imprint of Penguin Books for *How to Wean Your Baby*.

Charlotte now runs regular online webinars covering three core areas that her ideal customers most need help with: first steps, next steps and fussy eaters.[17]

Bespoke Betty

> Designed around primarily working one-to-one with clients, online or from a clinic. This is a time-for-money exchange: you make a certain number of hours available in your week and work with people in one-off sessions or on a programme of your own design which is delivered on calls or in-person.

> You will be a master of things like search engine optimisation and get found online by ideal customers without needing to 'launch' and promote a lot. Referrals are your bread and butter.

> Might involve carefully selected speaking engagements and PR to help position you as an expert in your field and bring in more bookings.

> May involve running a few free or paid one-off webinars or challenges to attract attention to your one-to-one work, particularly at the beginning when you are building a reputation. But eventually these will just be an added extra way to get sign ups, not as a necessity for your business model to work.

Pros

> Able to earn money immediately, no matter how small your audience.

> You will build up a knowledge of what your ideal customers want and need by working with them one-to-one, which means you *could* (if you want to), run a course or group programme later down the line, pulling the common threads and most useful tools together in a one-to-many offer.

> You don't have to relentlessly 'launch' or come up with new products and offerings. You'll have a constant suite of one-to-one packages that you refine over time, but that remain fairly continuous and feel like they 'sell themselves' when you've nailed producing content that connects and the referrals build.

Cons

> You will need to charge appropriately for your one-to-one packages to ensure you make the income you want. This isn't a 'con' necessarily, just something to consider –your money mindset and pricing need to match the model to make the income you desire.

> This is a slow burn, but solid way to build a business but it won't make you a millionaire overnight or result in big spikes of income. If you're looking for a big hit of money in one go this isn't the model for you.

CASE STUDY: EVE KALINIK

I came across Eve and her work when I attended a gut health talk hosted by *The Guardian* as part of their live events series.

Having first worked in fashion PR, Eve's fast-paced, high-profile job meant she started to suffer with gut health issues and recurrent infections which led her to seek help to change her diet and lifestyle. She spent three years studying and qualifying to become a Nutritional Therapist and now runs her own practice. The core of Eve's offer is her personal consultations – either online or in person from her Notting Hill practice. She specialises in gut health and digestive conditions including IBS and (Inflammatory Bowel Disease) IBD, as well as conditions linked to the gut, that include autoimmune diseases, mood disorders and skin issues.

Eve attracts clients to her practice through carefully selected speaking events (such as the one at *The Guardian* where I came across her) and more recently through her podcast *The Wellness Breakdown* with high-profile Functional Medicine Practitioner and model Rose Ferguson. Eve also hosts her own events and has published two books, all of which give her ample PR opportunities to get her work in front of new audiences through the media, which leads back to clients for her practice.[18]

Responder Rachel

> Revolves around you seeing what people need and then offering it in the form of courses, webinars, challenges, ebooks or courses.
> Is constantly evolving and adaptive. You will have offers at different price points to cater for your customers at each stage – right from cheap-as-chips and no brainer offers, through to a VIP level way of working with you in a more personalised way.
> Might have some evergreen (always available) products, such as a one-to-one offer. But everything else is new and changing to respond to demand.

Pros

> You will learn a huge amount about what people want, what works and what you enjoy by using this method.
> If you have a small audience, this is a great way to immediately provide what they are asking for and start to build a reputation as a problem solver and helpful practitioner.

Cons

> You will need to 'launch' and promote your new offers regularly. This isn't a con necessarily, just something to be aware of and to ensure you have the energy to operate in this way.

> It can be easy to confuse your audience if you try to launch and sell too many different things. Your offers need to be distinctive and well-spaced to allow your messaging to be clear and your audience to not feel overwhelmed by the options you're providing.

CASE STUDY: VICKY SHILLING

I very much started my business as a Bespoke Betty – one-to-one coaching and mentoring were the only ways to work with me. Over the last two years I have shifted more to a Responder Rachel business model to grow my audience and testing different products to learn what I enjoy and what helps my clients the best.

In response to the questions and problems I have seen my audience struggle with, I have over the last two years:

> Created free and paid for trainings
> Hosted free and paid for meet ups, online and in person

> ❭ Run bi-monthly online webinars on specific topics
> ❭ Opened an online shop to purchase access-anytime products
> ❭ Launched a membership
> ❭ Run a group programme
> ❭ Adapted and changed my one-to-one offerings to better cater for the needs of my audience

Testing out and trialling all these different models has given me data to make future decisions about the best products to proceed with and a community to talk to and design offers for in future.

Signature Sally

> Is designed around offering a signature long-running one-to-many course or membership, available to sign up to anytime or enrolling just once or twice a year, charged at a higher level.

> Requires total commitment to a single product that offers the solution to your customers' problems and results in big transformation and change.

> Can also generate income working one-to-one, but at a much higher level with a select number of people.

Pros

> Doesn't involve constant launching and selling different things all year round.

> Payment plans and consistent sign ups make this feel like a sustainable way to build a business, rather than peaks and troughs of launching balanced with quiet periods.

> Long-running support usually offers bigger transformation and change, so a bigger chance of happy customers as you give them the time and support they need to see results.

> Your 'signature' offer could be developed and built as you go – so you don't need to have hours of training and resources prepared before starting to sell. You can create as you go.

Cons

> Needs to be the right offer, which can take time and experience to put together and know how to articulate in a way that sells, something you most likely do not have immediately upon qualifying. If the content isn't right in your 'signature' offer, you risk unhappy customers. You need to be confident, if you onboard people to a long-running programme, that it will deliver. It's not the same as a one-off six- or eight-week course.

> Requires an established reputation of some sort and/or investment in paid advertising to get sign ups. Launching out of the blocks with a 'signature' offer is possible, but to get people to pay at a higher level for ongoing support requires trust from your customers and extremely good marketing copy – neither of which may be your natural strength as a newly-qualified practitioner.

CASE STUDY: SANDRA GREENBANK

I came across Sandra as her name was mentioned by multiple clients as someone who offers a signature course that they wanted to emulate. Her journey is a perfect example of a Signature Sally.

A Registered Nutritional Therapist, Sandra studied for four years at the Institute of Optimum Nutrition and qualified in 2009. Having worked for over a decade one-to-one within her specialist area, fertility, Sandra identified the key pillars of support that she offered each of her private clients and was able to turn this into a signature offer: her Fertility Foundations Programme.

Covering nourishment, lifestyle, supplements, Q&As, a community, resources and discounts, Sandra has made her programme into a purchase anytime product that comes with a community of previous graduates who can support and encourage one another.

She's been able to design this highly impactful course through helping multiple clients over several years so that she knows that (and no doubt continues to refine) the course content gets results. As she's established her reputation, the course and her website rank well on Google for searches like 'online nutrition fertility programme'.

As a result of this programme, she has now reached a position in her business where she has chosen not to work with one-to-one clients herself any longer.

Instead, she has put together a team of certified fertility experts who can teach and share her ethos and method. This a choice she can make having established a solid standing and enquiry stream through many years of work and delivery of her programme.[19]

Which business model archetype best fits you?

Take my quiz to find out which business model suits you, based on your personality and how you want to shape your work life.

Access the quiz by downloading the resources for the book at
www.juststartnowbook.vickyshilling.com

You'll be matched with your ideal archetype and given a free training to get you started.

How do I decide what to offer?

Fundamentally whether you plump for one of these archetypes or a blend of them, what you offer should be determined by two things:

1. What gets your customers the best outcome? (That is always where we ground from and where great, genuinely helpful businesses thrive.)
2. How you like to work with people, the business model that brings you joy and plays to your strengths.

When you create a business that has maximum impact and utilises your natural abilities and preferences, selling and making money becomes so much easier, rather than forcing yourself into a cookie-cutter 'I have to make money like this' plan.

What suits your personality?

Now it might be that you're reading this and nodding along and getting it all in theory. Yup, I can see the logic in these business models, Vicky.

But a whole lot of questions keep coming up.

If I've never done this before, how do I know what my preference is when it comes to how to work?

How do I know if I'll like working with people one-to-one, or prefer groups? How do I know if I will love doing webinars if I've never done one before?

I hear you.

I would argue you do *and* you don't know.

Let's look at the fact that you probably do know what your preference is. Because you know your personality.

You've lived with yourself for a good few years now. You've noticed what you're drawn to. Where you excel. Where you get lost in the zone and lose hours because you're just *loving* what you're working on. Where you thrive talking to a person or multiple people. You *do* know what you like, if you're honest with yourself.

The problem is that we often don't tune into those preferences – the things we're inherently good at – and acknowledge our natural tendencies.

In fact, worse than just not tuning in, we mostly bull-doze over our innate way of working in a bid to be the most hustling, keeping-up-with-the-Joneses, 'masculine energy' version of ourselves we can muster, because we think that's what will make us successful.

But if we strip all that away, and look at how we would *like* to work, if money was no object and we didn't have to 'please' anyone else or hadn't been seduced by the latest shiny thing, you probably do know how you'd love things to go.

If you struggle to articulate or know what makes you tick, have you tried a personality test? A confessional at this stage: I am not on the surface of it a big fan of personality tests. That's because I feel they get people stuck into a fixed mindset of being unable to change and grow.

"Oh well, I've done an online Myers-Briggs Personality Test and I'm an INFJ so I'm a perfectionist and a people pleaser, that's just how I am."

Not helpful. I really believe you can identify traits and work to change or improve them (or just think about them differently) if you find they're holding you back.

After a session with my Just Start Now community with a guest Business Coach, Lucy Green, on building your business to suit your personality, I changed my mind a bit on testing.

Lucy identified two particular areas that, having observed now hundreds of people starting their own business, I can absolutely see people fall into. Lucy explains more:

"Knowing your preferences is so important! It's not about pigeonholing yourself, more understanding your strengths and finding your own ways of working that suit you best. Here are two traits to take into account when making business decisions.

Introverts versus Extroverts
Introversion is often confused with being shy, and extroversion connected with confidence – but this isn't the case. These traits are about where you get your energy from.

Introverts recharge their batteries alone, needing solo time to reflect, process and think. Extroverts get energy from being around others – bouncing off people they're with.

If you're an extrovert, working with groups and doing live events could suit you. You'll thrive working in-person or with an audience, rather than home alone.

If you're an introvert, then working one-to-one, designing self-paced courses or more 'hands-off' type support programmes would be a better fit for you.

Judging versus Perceiving

This trait is about structure and order. Either you love to be prepared and scripted, with a focus on clear deadlines and planning ahead (judging). Or you love to be spontaneous and flexible, get bored easily and prefer to keep your options open (perceiving)

If you're more judging, designing a limited suite of products and offers that are available over set time periods, with a clear start and end point, could suit you best.

If you're more perceiving, then being more reactive to your community and clients, and leaving your business model open to new courses and offers could suit you best."[20]

If you haven't before, and you don't really feel you can articulate your preferred working style, why not give a personality test a go? You can take one for free at www.16personalities.com

Personally, having had Lucy explain these different traits to me, I identify very much as an introvert – which you might not think to look at me or my content online! But I mostly get my energy and kicks from working on and planning content and training alone, rather than needing and craving contact with others.

I absolutely understand that I need to work with people and that live or online events and support *really* get my customers results so I make this part of the mix (because this isn't just about me, it's about my clients and achieving the outcomes they want too). However, my natural tendency is to find ways to plan and create resources away from others, so I make that integral to how I run my business.

When it comes to judging or perceiving I am 100% aligned to a more carefully judged way of working. I cannot bear spontaneity. Whilst I've been a Responder Rachel in the way I have grown my business, which you might think is perceiving, each of the different products have been carefully planned and delivered. No spur -of-the-moment decisions: my group programme was mapped out six months in advance of releasing it! It's what works for me and makes me feel good and secure in my business.

You must give *something* a go

The other thing to say about choosing your business model and which products and services you want to offer is you must try something, in order to know.

My Dad brought us up with the mantra, "You can't

say you don't like it until you've tried it", when it came to food. Maybe there was a similar philosophy in your household.

The same applies to business.

When it comes to deciding what the best product is to put out there and sell, all you can do is work from your best knowledge and know-how that you have in this moment. Taking on board how you feel, what is within your skill set and what serves the goals you've set yourself.

Giving something a go for *at least* 90 days is a great way to test something out and see how you feel about it. What have you got to lose? There's knowledge and learning to be gained by giving *something* a shot and seeing if you like it.

Is this really for you?

The final honest point I need to make here when it comes to business models and comparing yourself to other people, is this: turning your passion for health and wellness into a business may not be right for you. And that's okay.

Perhaps you've read through all of these business model suggestions and every one of them turns your stomach. There's nothing that says excitement and fun in them, nothing you want to give a go.

That's okay.

I know it might look from social media or when you

go to events that everyone is going solo, setting up their own practice, writing a thriving blog, running a YouTube channel and generally bossing being a boss.

This is not the case.

Some people cannot and will not ever thrive on the highs and lows, the ups and downs, the personal development journey and the insecurity that comes with working for yourself.

That's okay.

There is absolutely nothing wrong with knowing that, when it's all said and done, being a solopreneur is not your cup of tea.

The world needs all sorts of people. If everyone was entrepreneurial and running their own show, who would be manning the hospitals, clinics and GP surgeries, advising the brands and food companies or working in the gyms and studios? The whole ecosystem works because we are all different and all enjoy and prosper working in different ways.

Working for yourself is not the 'better' route. It's one route. It might be for you. It might not be for you.

What I don't want, though, is that you make the decision not to pursue your own health-based business out of fear.

You only have one life. I don't want you to go another 10 years, 20 years, and constantly look back and think, "What if I'd gone for it?"

Our brains are wired to think of all the worst-case scenarios when we do something new, such as stepping out into business alone. But the chances are you'll never look back and think you wish you *hadn't* gone for it. You'll wish you'd given it a shot and seen whether you were cut out for it, just to know.

As I've been writing this chapter an email dropped into my inbox asking about income possibilities when it comes to running a health coaching business.

Paraphrased, the email reads, "How much money is realistic to expect working in wellness? My partner is nervous about me giving up my secure, well-paid job, and we think there's only so long we could survive on one salary. I need to reassure him. What sort of figure can I say?"

My response?

The whole point of working for yourself is . . . earning potential is limitless.

You don't have a boss, you set your own prices, you promote and create as many products and services as you want and the only thing that holds you back is you.

But the thing for me to stress is, whilst limitless sounds amazing, it does take time. People buy from you when they know, like and trust you. That doesn't happen instantly.

If you've got the patience, the determination and you focus on the right things, and have the type of personality that loves creating your own offers and can roll with the ups and downs, it *will* work out for you. You must keep the faith.

Let's recap

1. Put on your blinkers when it comes to designing your business model. You never know the full story behind someone else's exterior.

2. Take one of the four business model archetypes as a starting point for imagining the type of business you want to build that plays to your strengths.

3. Tune into your personality to decide what business model is right for you. Pick something and give it a go for at least 90 days to see what you learn.

4. Running your own business might not be for you. If that's the case, that's okay. But don't make a decision purely from fear.

Stop thinking (notice)
> I'll never be successful like they are
> There's only one way to build a business
> I'm just not a good business person

Start thinking (flip to)
> There is a business model that suits me perfectly
> I earn money in a way that feels good to me
> People can't wait to buy my offer

6

Ethics and doing business the right way

The next hurdle to tackle is selling.

Gulp.

It's a big one. Now it's time to tackle the mindset blocks and stories you have right now about selling, making money and the hang ups you have about doing business.

And trust me, you and I might not have met yet. But I know you. And you have blocks and stories on these things. We all do. Myself included.

There is one common money story in particular that comes up for many of us. It should be no surprise. Just look at the business landscape we are heading into and see if you can spot it.

Wellness influencer De La Mare-Kenny used the fear and uncertainty of the early days of COVID-19 pandemic to promote a dietary supplement she sold through her website as a way to 'boost [your immune system] and make it bullet proof to Corona' to make fast money at the expense of her worried following, with no evidence or qualifications to do so.

Let's add to that fitness influencer Brittany Dawn Davis, who used her social media platform to sell her followers 'customized' personal coaching and nutrition plans costing up to $US300, but which customers complained were all the same.

At the other end of the entrepreneurial scale? Jeff Bezos sits on a billion dollar fortune while his Amazon warehouse workers are subjected to 'dehumanising' working conditions, high injury rates, relentless 'robot-like' output targets and 15-minute breaks that barely leave enough time to visit a bathroom.

And let's not forget Elizabeth Holmes, the world's first self-made female billionaire. She grew her company, Theranos, by claiming she had a technology that could run hundreds of tests on a single drop of blood, yet has now been found guilty of fraud as the tech she claimed to have never actually existed.

It all boils down to a single message we get about doing business.

Making money means you're a bad person

De La Mare-Kenny? *Trading on fear.*

Brittany Dawn Davis? *Liar*

Jeff Bezos? *Doesn't care about his staff*

Elizabeth Holmes? *Fraud*

Every week we see online, and hear in the news, stories just like this. The kind of big bucks earners who are selling, charging, promoting, exploiting staff and followers and using their money in a way that is frankly abhorrent to an ethical way of living, something I *know* is important to you.

If we use these examples as our benchmark, earning money and having a comfortable lifestyle always appear to come at a cost.

These headlines tell us and our inner critic one thing: someone has to suffer if we get paid.

But this is not true.

And the problem is, if we take on these headlines as universal business truths and believe that earning money makes you a bad person, here's what happens:

1. We set our prices based on what we think people can afford, rather than taking into consideration what we want and need to earn.

2. We give things away rather than charging our full worth, leaving us feeling undervalued.

3. We avoid selling and promoting ourselves for fear that we'll become a horrible money-grabbing nasty if we make cash from what we do.

4. We live in a continuing cycle of earning no money and helping no one, only further eroding our confidence.

I do not want this cycle for you.

So let me affirm and change your mind: it is safe to make money.

It is *good* that you make money. You can make money *and* have a positive impact in the world. You can make money, create a wonderful life for yourself *and* do good in the world.

You can make money, sell in a way that feels great, create a wonderful life for yourself *and* do good in the world.

These aspirations are not mutually exclusive.

A powerful yet simple language switch I'm demonstrating here, that can be employed in any area of your life and business to huge positive effect, is to swap out the word 'or' for the word 'and'.

The word 'or' is a form of scarcity: if I have *this*, then it means I have to go without *that*. If I get what *I* want, then it means someone else will struggle, it's me *or* them.

'Or' comes from zero-sum thinking: an evolutionary flaw we're stuck with that means our brains tell us if someone else is thriving, we will suffer, or vice versa. Back in the cave, thousands of years ago, that might have been true if someone else was scoffing all the mammoth meat. But in the modern age? There is enough to go around for everyone.

We need to override that cave person part of our brains.

Let's embrace the abundance of *and* – instead of the lack of *or*.

When it comes to earning it's not, "I can make money *or* have a positive impact in the world." It's "I can make money *and* have a positive impact in the world." It's not "I can sell in a way that feels great to me *or* make great sustainable money." It's "I can sell in a way that feels great to me *and* make great sustainable money."

I'm not saying switching up your language is going to magically end the scammy ways of wellness influencers or make the world's billionaires behave responsibly.

But what it will do is remind you that making money and caring about people are both things you can have in your life and work. Together. Simultaneously.

You can be that brilliant example to others.

Because people who earn well, do great things too.

In 2021, there were over 3,500 companies worldwide who are Certified B Corporations – businesses that work towards reduced inequality, lower levels of poverty, a healthier environment and stronger communities. Businesses genuinely doing good.

In fact, visiting senior lecturer at Yale School of Management, Professor Henrietta Onwuegbuzie, argues that if we go back to their roots, businesses were always meant to help people, not just make cash:

"We ... believe that you set up a business to make money while nonprofits, charities, and government are meant to concern themselves with impacting lives. However, business can be a tool for social transformation, while remaining profitable, and we're losing sight of this.

...

Impact-driven businesses make money while making a difference because they impact lives. They therefore bridge the gap between economic growth and social development, by creating shared prosperity and consequently a better, safer world."[21]

Making money should be the best possible way to make an impact.

Let's see ourselves as impact-driven business owners. Selling and earning for good, not just for ourselves.

If we don't, we'll never get comfortable with selling.

Selling is the ultimate act of kindness

Here's another reframe to help you embrace the sales process. Earning money is the most generous and kind thing you can possibly do for other people.

How so?

I love to think about how earning money makes me far *more* likely to be able to give to charity and donate generously than if I just keep giving away my courses, programmes and time for free, or on the cheap. The same goes for you too.

If you're struggling to pay the bills, are you in a position to give a scholarship place on your next group programme or donate when you see a cause you love in need? Probably not.

But if you were a consistent earner, how much and how often could you give?

Weekly? Monthly? Annually? A percentage of your annual revenue? Randomly when the desire takes you or when you find a charity doing brilliant work? If you knew the money was coming in, could you give up a day to volunteer with a cause you feel passionate about?

Hell, if you were earning really well you could even set up your own charity if that would float your boat. Imagine! What's more generous and caring than that?

I coached Helen on a group programme once who knew that her bigger mission was to buy land to rewild and support biodiversity with the money she was going to earn from her hypnotherapy business helping people with Irritable Bowel Syndrome (IBS). She even highlights this higher purpose on her website alongside the partner organisation she donates to that plants global tropical forests.[22] What a great motivator to keep going out and filling her programmes – the benefits of Helen earning were going to ripple even beyond the IBS sufferers she supported.

If you would love to be charitable with your earnings then selling, making money and charging appropriately is an incredibly generous and kind thing to do. Think about it like that.

Investing gets results

Finally, let's stick one last nail in the coffin of "earning money makes me a bad person".

I'm a big believer that when people invest, they get a great return. That's because they take seriously what you are offering – they commit, to you *and* themselves. When they've paid appropriately for your offer they take action, they show up and they do the work.

When you are being paid properly for your time and experience, you as a practitioner also show up and give your clients your time and attention more fully – because they've paid a price that is aligned with your worth, your expertise and the transformation they're going to get from working with you. It changes your attention and commitment, and everyone benefits.

The people you give freebies to, that you do a mates rates deal for, that you down sell and knock off money for – they're not the people who are going to do the work. They're not committed, and neither are you in quite the same way.

If anything, you're left feeling pretty resentful and bitter about having to do the work for such a low rate. I've seen it happen over and over again.

Charlotte, who came through one of my programmes, was a highly qualified pharmacist and herbalist who had never been able to break the cycle of giving away free advice constantly. Her social media channel, supposedly her means of marketing herself and getting paying clients, became a one-stop shop for anyone to pick her brains in her direct messages. It was leaving her feeling resentful and exasperated that she would never be able to create the income she wanted if all anyone ever wanted from her was free tips.

In this situation? No one's winning. No one's getting great outcomes. The person getting the freebie doesn't get the results they want. Because they don't truly value the advice or act on it. And Charlotte feels totally under-valued and aggrieved at giving them everything for little to no return.

It wasn't until we turned things around for Charlotte and helped her get clear on her offer, her messaging and switched up her belief systems, that she started to get paid for what she was great at. Coming through my programme, she launched her first ever online talk and within 24 hours she had already sold half the places. The first money she'd ever earned in her fledgling business.

With all this in mind, is it possible for you to think that by earning what you want, you are actually helping *more* people, rather than fewer people?

Can you see that by charging your worth you're helping people in a deeper and more impactful way? That by selling something you are allowing people the *joy* of investing in you and getting the transformation they so crave? Can you start to believe that when there's a fair exchange of need and skill, everyone wins?

And let me also add that cash is, of course, not the only currency. The principle here is that people feel *invested* in some way and that what you offer is not just a one-way transaction where you give it all and they take it. If it's not money, what can the exchange be so that you feel compensated and rewarded for what you have shared, instead of feeling like you've been taken advantage of?

Selling without the shady tactics

Now we've put that money story to bed, let's get back to selling.

Here's the thing. Selling and sales are dirty words to many of us. And that's because we're trained to hate sales people and their slimy sales tactics.

Is it any wonder, with the examples we see around us?

I remember my sister once went for a photoshoot in London. It was one of these shoots that, on the surface of it, looks like a bargain girls day out. Low investment to get dressed up with your best friend, get your hair and make-up done and then get a range of photos in different set ups. It was fun and the photos looked great. The photographer flicked through them on a screen and showed my sister and her friend – were they going to buy some?

That's when it turned nasty and the shady sales tactics came in. The photos were pricey compared with the small investment of turning up for the shoot. There were different deals that the photographer fired at them as he scrolled through the pictures – you can buy them all, or there's this price for 10, or how about three for a great offer?

My sister and her friend were just teenagers – they didn't have the kind of money the photographer was talking. They ummed and ahhed and questioned what to do.

And the photographer? He kept laying on the pressure. Time was ticking, he needed to get to his next shoot. Were they going to make a decision? No? Not sure? Oh well . . . I'll just have to delete them . . .

Panicked as they saw their favourite snaps disappearing from the screen as he cruelly deleted them to push them into a sale, they agreed to a package they couldn't really afford. Someone had a credit card – they'd put it on that and explain to parents when they got home.

The whole fun day out had been soured by the buying experience. A pushy salesperson, tricking them using nasty tactics into buying something they couldn't really afford and perhaps didn't really want, had got his way and they were left feeling remorseful and vulnerable.

"I felt pressured and like I had no option. I paid and felt so immensely guilty and sick about how much I'd spent I hid the CD with the photos on it and didn't look at them for years. It gave me a knot in the pit of my stomach just thinking about it," my sister said when I asked her about it.

Who the hell wants to be a salesperson if *this* is your role model of how to make sales?

It's become accepted that being a sales person simply *must* be the worst part of anyone's job. And if you're going to open your own business? Sales has pretty much *got* to be a part of what you do in some shape or form. Which can bring many of us out in hives just thinking about it. We'd love to just be brilliant at what we do and not have to ever 'sell' a thing.

Once again, just like the bad examples of successful, money-earning business owners, bad sales people are the ones that stick in our minds and give us poor role models for what it means to 'sell' in our business.

> Pushy and relentless
> Self-promoting and always on broadcast/transmit
> Using underhand, manipulative tactics

Selling doesn't have to be that way. In fact I'd argue it should never be this way. Let's flip how you think about sales.

What does good selling look like?

Good selling is the art of great listening. Of grounding yourself in conversation and truly absorbing what your ideal customers are saying they need. And then giving it to them.

Ultimately if good selling is great listening, sales is about being clear on what you're selling. It's about great communication.

And what you're selling isn't the package, the workbook, the testing, the meal plans, the notes you send your clients. It's not even your amazing knowledge or qualifications.

It's the outcome, the result, the transformation that the customer is going to get when they invest in what you've put together for them.

That's what they get. That's what they are buying.

And when you can get really clear and confident at articulating that, selling ceases to become about bigging yourself up and highlighting all your amazing attributes continuously (gross), and instead is a genuine flow of conversation and solving people's problems. Which I know is what you want.

How to sell in a way that feels good

If we know that a) making money is great for everyone, b) what we're really selling is the outcome the customer will get and, c) sales is really just the art of conversation, how then do we sell in a way that feels good and aligned?

Here's what I *don't* think selling is.

> Charging huge high prices because a business guru told you to
> Being pushy or using sales techniques that make you feel uncomfortable, like insisting on taking a deposit on a call or asking potential customers if they can take out a credit card to pay you if they don't have the cash right now
> Relentless cycles of 'launching' and being visible, live and in sales mode, which are unsustainable and exhausting for you on an ongoing basis

> Using scarcity and fear of missing out (FOMO) tactics constantly, or fictionalising scarcity to drive sales
> Offering free events with the promise of juicy information, that wind up having no actionable substance and are really just one long sales pitch

If there is any sales methodology you have witnessed or been taught that doesn't sit right, you don't have to do it.

You have my total permission to sell in a way that feels good for you. Take this permission slip and breathe a big sigh of relief.

Just as we talked in Chapter 5 about choosing a business model that works for you and your strengths, finding a way to sell on an ongoing basis that feels enjoyable is key to having a successful business. There are no 'shoulds' when it comes to selling.

Naturally, there will be some methods that get quicker or bigger results. But you need to stop and question – what kind of business am I building here?

Because trust me, I've seen the people going all guns blazing on the 'quick results' methods. And, for most, it's exhausting, ends in burn-out and anxiety, and does not create the stable, consistent income that I *know* you're craving.

My only caveat, however, when it comes to finding your way to sell is this: you do have to do it. I'm afraid selling is a non-negotiable.

Even if you hired in a salesperson to fill your pipeline (and I'm guessing that's not something you can readily afford as you're just starting out, but let's pretend), you will still have to 'sell' during the course of running your business. You will have to talk to people about what you do in a positive way that inclines them to buy from you or recommend you.

You are your business. Even if you're planning something bigger than a solopreneur venture, people buy from people. They want to see your enthusiasm and your clarity about the customers you serve and the solution you're offering.

Tesla has 12 million followers on Twitter, Elon Musk has 63 million. What does that tell you about how people are influenced into buying?

Your own personal brand is so important. You as the business owner are actually doing the selling. People buy from people.

So when it comes to selling, if it's not the shady tactics we *thought* were sales, what's left?

> Having genuine conversations with people (whether that's in person, on email or in direct messages or voice notes)
> Promoting and being visible in a way that matches with your strengths, your energy and your values
> Trusting that dream clients are watching everything you say and do and *will* come, you just need to keep showing up (more on that in Chapter 10)
> Allowing people to think about it and get back to you when the time's right instead of forcing a sale

Trust that dream clients are watching everything you say and do and will come, you just need to keep showing up.

Obviously there's more skill and detail when it comes to the art of great selling than just these four bullet points, but we do not have space for that here. But I hope I'm leaving you with the clarity and endorsement to ditch the get-rich-quick selling methods and embrace ways that you can genuinely imagine incorporating into your working life on a weekly, if not daily basis. (Yes, sales needs to be happening that often!)

You have the permission slip now. You can sell in a way that feels good for you *and* make great money.

The ethics of selling

And so what we are teetering on the brink of now is the question of business ethics.

The whole question of ethical selling, particularly in the world of wellness, reminds me so vividly of watching a horrifying documentary back in 2017, around the time of the backlash against the phrase 'clean eating'. The TV programme focused on a charlatan practitioner who took money from terminal cancer patients promising them a cure through the 'Gerson regimen', feeding his clients a diet of crushed fruit and vegetables only as a way to 'heal' them. He administered the 'treatments' as the patients died slowly, away from the medical support that would have aided them and eased their pain, and sometimes away from their families and loved ones, having spent their life savings on flying to his 'exclusive' centre to receive the supposed life-saving juice tonics.

This type of deception is not isolated. Do you remember Belle Gibson, the influencer who lied about having cancer in order to get a cookbook deal with book publisher Penguin and an app backed by tech giant Apple?

Not one of us wants to be seen like these people, or any of the other number of offenders who trick their customers when it comes to selling what we do.

But the fear that you will somehow be tarred with the same brush is where I find paralysis can come in.

The more you as a practitioner look at what's going on out there, the more you question what you're doing and if it's even possible to do it ethically.

You see more and more people doing questionable things when it comes to selling. You don't want to be grouped with them – it's better to quit and avoid any possible association, right?

I've been there.

Just as my business was taking off, a well-known business coach was hit by a big scandal. Accusations went flying around about the ethics of what they were doing – accusations of emotionally manipulative sales tactics, shouty messages about bigger and bigger financial goals, flashing Rolex watches and Bentley cars that raised alarm bells . . .

The situation sent me into a tailspin. It created such a negative energy in the coaching world. The hurt and mistrust that arose was ugly to watch and depressing for those of us in the same field who don't use the same tactics or conform to the same business approach.

I didn't want to be associated with the 'business coaching' industry if this is what people saw and thought of us.

If I was going to be lumped with coaches who were being accused of lying, deceiving and giving a poor service, I didn't want to do this at all.

So I get how you're feeling, I really do.

When there are genuine cheats and con artists out there, you don't want to be associated with them.

But please believe me when I say: you won't be. Because I truly believe you're different. Just as I came to the realisation *I* was different. I was needed and I continued doing my work.

Because remember what we said in Chapter 3 about real imposters not thinking they're imposters?

The same is true here.

If you are agonising and tying yourself up in knots about business ethics and whether your prices are right, whether it's okay for you to earn a profit, take home good money, charge for your knowledge, see a financial exchange in order to improve people's health, if you really can get people the outcome they want from your work, guess what?

You're an ethical business owner.

Because even stopping to think for five seconds about any of these questions means you are putting the happiness and satisfaction of your customers above your own business and personal interests.

You're not the same as someone who will swindle and rip off their customers for their own gain. You are customer-focused and prioritise caring about their outcomes over and above your own.

You're the kind of practitioner the world needs.

Please, please don't stop.

People need you.

Let's recap

1. Making money does not make you a bad person. In fact, charging your worth and earning well is better for everyone – you're more able to be generous with your time and cash and the people who invest get better results. Win win.

2. Selling is the art of conversation, not the art of being pushy. Enjoy talking and showing genuine interest and you'll make more sales.

3. What you are selling is not your time, your skill or the amazing factsheets you've put together. It's the results, the outcome you get your customers. The quicker you can get clear on articulating that, the more sales will come easily.

4. You have total permission to reject any and all sales tactics that make you feel icky and gross. Find a way to sell that feels good for you.

5. You are not an unethical business owner if you make money. Read that again.

Stop thinking (notice)

> Making money is bad
> Selling is pushy
> It's impossible to earn money and be ethical

Start thinking (flip to)

> Everyone benefits when I earn
> I can make money *and* have a positive impact in the world
> I am different. I am needed

7

Society and privilege

It would be remiss of me to continue this book, happily giving out my tips about how simple and possible it is to rewire your brain for more positivity and start to 'just start now' taking action in your fledgling business, without acknowledging a few home truths about the world we're operating in.

Because the sad fact is, we aren't all operating from the same level playing field.

As much as we are sold the 'if I can do it, you can too' story, sadly that's too simplistic.

And I'll be honest, I did that for a long time.

I genuinely thought that pointing out the mindset blocks and suggesting methods and ways to change your thinking could be the answer alone. Once you had those juicy nuggets of my wisdom, you'd suddenly do the thing! Right?!

It wasn't until I started on my own path into anti-racism work, and began to experience in my own life kickbacks and comments about my appearance, that I started to realise – we don't all get the same opportunities. We are, sadly, not all viewed the same. Which means that rightly or wrongly, the businesses we dream of creating have different levels of success due to factors beyond our control.

All the action and 'just starting now' in the world cannot, sometimes, override what have become societal norms and standards that we are expected to conform to and that dictate how we are received in the world.

So instead of blindly continuing like we're all beginning together from the same start line, I want to take a moment to identify and come to terms with some of the wider, societally-embedded reasons you might not feel you're able to 'just start now' whilst someone else is.

Because there's nothing wrong with you. At all. In fact, there's everything right with you. We just need an honest look at why we're getting stuck or making slower progress than the next person, through no fault of our own.

I want to touch on these blocks in three areas:

1. Body discrimination
2. Hidden privilege
3. Racism

Body discrimination

During Dietitians Week 2021, UK-based Australian Registered Dietitian Dotti Balhatchet shared a post on her Instagram account, "Being a fat dietitian feels harder when we are left out of the conversation about diversity in the profession".[23]

In the post she explained articulately how hurtful it was that whilst diversity was starting to be more openly discussed and encouraged in the dietetics industry, it seemed that some still, despite all their knowledge, science and training, could not look past the fact she was fat.

To many of her colleagues, when she had been a thin graduate with 'questionable eating habits', she was somehow a better practitioner than the 15-year-more-experienced, yet heavier, version of herself. Her voice was less valued as her weight grew.

Body discrimination is rife in society, but it's gutting to realise that even people who are educated to understand the biology of human metabolism and who treat daily people of all shapes and sizes, still interact in a way with their co-workers that displays the stigma and assumptions that linger in wider society where there is less education.

This is a stark reminder of how deep-rooted the stories and messages are about how a person's weight is somehow linked to their character and abilities.

And it's not only Dotti's experience, it has come up in my own too.

Having been for many years a fairly typical and societally accepted UK size 10–12, after giving birth to my daughter in 2020, I was naturally carrying a few more pounds than I had ever done before.

Feeling very blessed to have surrounded myself with an online and offline world of people advocating a positive relationship with my body, feeling awe and admiration for the fact it had grown and pushed out a human, and loved and supported by family and friends who had never made a comment, I posted an Instagram Reel (short video) promoting my latest course a few months after my maternity leave without a second thought.

The video was all about how to start a sustainable business. I danced around to 'This is how we do it' by Montell Jordan and pointed out my five tips as they popped up in text on the screen.

After a couple of hours of the video being live, a comment was left by an account I didn't know. 'And stop eating?! Lol'

I've never been trolled before. Not if we don't count the person who once said a photo of my recipe for tofu chocolate mousse looked like "someone just pooped in a glass".

At first I was a bit confused about what the comment on my video meant. And then it hit.

He was implying I needed to lose weight.

His assumption was, upon seeing my body dancing in the video, that I must have a problem with controlling my urges around food. That clearly from the look of me, I was binging on biscuits between filming and had 'let myself go'. And that what was really important was for him to point out that he thought this and give me some funny/helpful/not-so-friendly advice on how to fix my 'problem'.

Suddenly all the stuff that we say about body positivity and diet culture came into sharp focus for me in a way that it hadn't before.

It became even more clear to me how difficult it is to be visible and show up in today's judgemental world.

This. This thing that had just happened to me, this man's comment. This is what so many of you are scared of.

Some of you live in fear that this exact situation (or worse) is what is going to happen if I suggest you share photos and videos of yourself, network, get a photoshoot done or whatever else it is that involves being seen in your business.

And that fear paralyses you into hiding, staying unseen behind stock images and snaps of landscapes, never being truly seen and taking up the space you deserve.

The biggest issue for me and Dotti, and perhaps you too, is that society associates certain body differences with being 'less than' at your job. And when you are promoting your own business and want to be recognised as an expert at what you do, this preconception totally undermines you.

The thing that most aggrieves me about these opinions about my appearance is that I *am* good at my job, as I have no doubt Dotti is, as I have no doubt you are too. And that's because our size has nothing to do with it.

I want to add that I'm no stranger to the idea that people who have smaller, slimmer bodies also struggle with their body image and being visible too and may well also receive unwelcome comments.

Or maybe for you it's your skin, your age, perhaps even a disability. I've had a client before where it was the depth of her wrinkles that stopped her showing her face on camera.

We all have hang ups because we've been taught to fixate on our bodies if we do not conform to the accepted look that society has developed for us. We learn to feel shame when we witness regular attacks on others with bodies like that, who have had the audacity to be seen.

Whatever your version of 'I don't look right' is, I see you. But as tough as it is, we have to move past this in order to be successful in business.

I'm not a perfect role model. That comment on my Instagram video stung. I wouldn't be human if it didn't hurt a little to be confronted by what negative things people think of me when they see my body.

But what I want to say to you is the same thing I said to myself in order to dust myself off and keep going after the comment.

Firstly, this is very rare. It is *not* the norm to receive sarcastic, passive aggressive comments on your content.

On the whole we must focus on the fact that the world is a kind and wonderful place and people value honesty and authenticity. Seeing you is important.

What we focus on expands – so let's look at all the good that happens when we share and show up. Not the tiny, tiny minority of people that think it's appropriate to pass judgement on what we look like on public forums.

At the point I posted that video to Instagram I had used the app for nearly four years continuously and shared at least 850+ pictures and videos. This was the first time this had happened.

Secondly, we cannot, I repeat cannot, be held back from being seen, saying what we need to say and from *helping people* with our amazing content and presence, because there *might* be someone out there who has a negative opinion about us.

Instead, as with everything we do, it's important to focus on our ideal customers and what *they* need to hear from us and see of us on any given day, not be held back by those who will never benefit from what we offer.

And thirdly, we have to look at the bigger picture here. The reason we have these fears and the reason that people pass judgement on how we look (whether they say it out loud or think it in their heads) is because of the diet-heavy culture we live in.

I know that many of you reading this will be true advocates for an inclusive, anti-diet, intuitive approach to health and wellbeing. As much as you fight against diet-culture for your clients, remember you must also role model rejecting it through the way you show up in your business.

The subliminal message buried within diet-culture is that we need to conform and look a certain way to be accepted, trusted and listened to as an authority. And

Don't be held back from helping people because someone might have a negative opinion about you.

believe me I know how that makes you feel. This is coming from a girl who started a healthy eating food blog in 2016, peak 'clean eating': the skinny, white, young, stunning 'health gurus' era. When I first stepped into this healthy living world there was a clear correlation between how you looked in a bikini with your smoothie bowl and your authority and ability to get a book deal. So I get you.

But let's all just accept in this moment now I've spelled it all out, that this is bullsh*t. And that if we want to fight that way of thinking and be part of any sort of resistance to body discrimination, that we need to show up as ourselves *despite* what might be said and thrown at us.

I'm not saying it's easy to go against what we've seen around us and tried to conform to all our lives. It's a life-long, societal imprint that runs deep.

But realising that our voices, our words, our knowledge and ability, are far more important and necessary to publish than conforming and playing small, is a mindset we simply *have* to cultivate. For ourselves *and* the people we want to help.

Hidden privilege

As I approached the end of the first year of working as a coach, beginning to work with clients while juggling a part-time job and setting up a wellness retreat business at the same time (I love to be busy!), I logged onto social media to see a large number of people I followed all posting from the same event in London.

It was being run by another coach and some of my previous clients, as well as followers who I had hoped might become *my* own clients, were attending.

The event looked buzzing. Tables of chatting people, brightly-dressed, glamorous coach host, luxury hotel meeting room surroundings and glowing comments and hashtags being shared about how #inspiring and #amazing the day had been.

Naturally, I did what we all do when we're staring down the slippery slope of comparison – I started to have a good nosey around this coach's account to find out what she was all about.

There was one, stand-out message to her marketing:

"In just one year I went from being a teacher to making $USD100,000."

Oof. That was hard to read.

It was December and after a year of working really hard at all three of my income generators (coaching, retreats and part-time music job), I was still facing a Christmas struggling to pay for gifts for my family and flights home to the UK. This woman had made six figures in just 12 months. What the *hell* was I doing wrong?

I share openly and honestly on my social media and so I turned to my Instagram to tell my followers what I'd just seen and how it had made me feel. One follower responded, "You never know the full story."

And that is so true. Sad, but true.

When we see someone's shiny, outward success, what we don't see is:

> The partner with a great job that covers all expenses and enables freedom to make mistakes with no financial cost
> The investment of $US100,000 in an expensive coach and shedloads of online advertising spend in order to bring in $USD100,000 (making a profit of $USD0)
> The highly-trained support on tap for free – maybe a best friend is a branding designer or a talented copywriter so they're already ahead
> The network and nepotism born into or built, maybe through education or previous work or just daddy's golf buddies that have opened doors and made the path easier

It's sad because these hidden privileges are often not shared. And this sends completely and utterly the wrong message to people like you and me starting out in business. We look on without the full story and think, "I must be a failure, I'm not getting those sorts of results."

But I am not a failure.

And you are not a failure.

The amount of time it is taking you to grow and build what will be your fabulous income source is the norm.

What is not the average experience is the exception who is supposedly fast-tracking to six figures in 12 months. Or less. I've seen business coaches claim they can get you from zero idea to six-figure earning in six weeks in some cases. That is not possible for the majority of us.

If we draw a comparison between this rapid business growth phenomenon and health, it's a bit like the 'eat like me, look like me' brigade.

No matter how many 'what I eat in a day' videos you watch, following the exact diet of Gisele Bündchen for the rest of your life will not make you the Boobs from Brazil.

In the same way, you could take all the same actions and make all the same investments as someone else with the business success you would like to emulate, but still get different results. Because you don't have the same hidden privileges they do.

The transparency of someone like Vogue Williams, who when asked, "how did you snap back into shape after giving birth?" said, "It's purely down to my body type that I went back to how I was before without too much effort"[24] is what we need in the world of business. We need honesty and transparency about what you have been gifted with that makes achieving something others long for easier for you.

When asked, "How did you make your first $USD100,000?" we should hear, "A lot of mistakes, a lot of time, a lot of tears and doubts and fears, and a huge amount of support and investment" rather than, "Oh I just followed this really simple plan and here I am – anyone can do it!"

The other important side to this more honest response is the hardships.

Rather than concealing the reality and making everything seem easy and effortless (which it can look from the shiny, social media friendly exterior), it's important to remember that whilst we all have hidden privilege, we also face difficulties that more business coaches and mentors should be open about.

Some would say that this isn't wise. That in order to motivate people to action, you should disguise and hide the struggle.

If you want to inspire someone to feel healthier and stronger in their bodies, overcome their digestive symptoms, do a pull-up, shake their anxiety, whatever it might be, do you tell them it's going to be tough and will take time?

I find it hard sometimes to strike a balance between honesty and inspiration in my own content. Between 'this has been tough' and 'you can do it!'. Because I believe both statements co-exist.

But I have told my clients and community that:

> It took me over a year to start making good sustainable income in my business
> I don't always hit my goals
> I struggle with comparison

> I go through quiet months where no one books and I get the wobbles
> I've launched things that have flopped

I think, overall, people value the honesty and reality of what it takes to be a solopreneur. They value the transparency about the hard work and years of under-earning or not earning at all and the failed businesses that have gone before, so that they feel hopeful that they can do it too. That the signs they might previously have thought meant they were 'failing' and 'not cut out for this' are actually things that higher-earning people have moved through successfully and these signs mean they're on the right path.

We cannot be what we cannot see.

If all we see are shiny success stories without the full background, we will be doomed to believe that running our own business is not possible if we ever stumble, trip or find it hard. And that is not true.

Make sure to surround yourself with a balanced, realistic vision of what it takes to be a business owner. Not just the glowing successes, whose full story you never really know.

Anti-racism and diversity

2020 was a year like no other, I think we can all agree. Added to the incredible global upheaval of the pandemic, I discovered I was pregnant at the end of February 2020.

The world was in lockdown. It actually suited me nicely in my first trimester – I could fake drink G&Ts on Zoom quiz nights without anyone getting suspicious and I didn't have to explain to anyone why I was no longer eating my beloved sushi. Because we weren't seeing anyone in person.

I was using this isolation time working away on my business, knowing that all being well, baby would be with us by the end of the year. I wanted and needed to earn as much money as I could before going off on maternity leave and so I got my head down, worked hard to follow all the steps my coach gave me and poured all my energy (when not napping) into my work.

And then the Black Lives Matter (BLM) protests began.

If we are looking for reasons to believe in the positive force of social media, a tool so often slammed as a negative and destructive presence in our lives, then I would argue what happened during the BLM protest period is a great example.

I'm not talking the black squares that were shared mindlessly by celebs and accounts that had done no work to understand the situation and did nothing to spread education or awareness.

I'm talking about the incredible content that was produced by black activists, coaches and educators to teach and explain to people like me what living a black life is really like in societies built to prioritise white people.

I'm talking about the ceaseless sharing that was done during BLM (and was happening well before and has continued well after) by diversity campaigners who were already tired of having to answer yet another white person asking, "But what am I supposed to do to help black people?"

I learned so much from what was shared during those weeks about my white privilege. The stories, the quotes, the statistics, the examples that were posted and re-posted were confronting and difficult to accept. But so necessary to hear and absorb. Suddenly the anti-racism work I knew I wanted to do but was always an 'I'll get round to it one day 'item on my to-do list, became this is work that I cannot delay any longer.

It was not only necessary for me to learn (or, some might say, try to un-learn) about racism for myself, my business and my clients in that moment. It was hugely important to me to do the work as a soon-to-be mother. As someone bringing yet another white-privileged human into the world. I couldn't bear the idea that my ignorance or unwillingness to address and dismantle my racist views and presumptions was going to pass on to her if I didn't do this work.

As an advocate for taking action and getting things done in your wellness business, what education I have managed to give myself in the area of racism has shown me that I must acknowledge something many would prefer to ignore.

It is infinitely easier for me to grow a business as a white woman than it is for a black person or person of another minority group.

And as a result of owning that fact, I must ensure that advantage is acknowledged to my audience and potential clients *and* use the platform I am creating to help make change in the world to benefit people of all skin colours and backgrounds, in whatever way I can.

If you identify as anything other than white and are looking to operate your wellness business in white-majority, western society, I see you (though of course I don't know exactly what you experience).

Racism holds black people and people from BAME backgrounds back from being amazing wellness practitioners because of the biases people have and the way western society is constructed, right down to the laws and systems that disproportionately affect people of colour.

Which means 'just follow my steps' won't wash here.

Until such a time as we reach a truly equitable society, your ability to 'just start now' could well be impaired by racism and prejudice from the society in which we live. I wish it wasn't. But there's no point pretending it doesn't exist.

I cannot share direct experience of being on the wrong side of systemic racism. So I wanted to introduce you to a friend and fellow business owner Nicola Rae-Wickham who brilliantly articulates what it feels like to run her business in this society and what words of advice she has for you if this is your reality:

"We all know that starting your own business is a huge personal development journey. As a black British woman I am well versed in navigating spaces that weren't made for me – from higher education to climbing the corporate ladder – and the wellness/coaching space was no different.

As a young girl the notion of working twice as hard for half as much was ever-present alongside the assertion that there is only ever room for one of us. These narratives (amongst others) co-exist in a difficult and perplexing position of being both truths of which I can bring copious amounts of evidence and lived experience, whilst also being truths which I intentionally seek to reimagine, challenge and dismantle as I live and work out loud.

In short, it is complex and that's what being a black or person from a historically marginalised community is like.

So when it comes to starting or growing a business, following your purpose and taking action, a nuanced approach rooted in understanding of the context is required.

For me, it looked like a deep exploration into how systemic racism has impacted how and why I did not and have not shown up as myself.

This then led to an unravelling of the survival mechanisms underpinned by editing, filtering, code switching and assimilating. Which in turn makes way for owning who you are, being open and honest about the specific challenges, calling out the unjust practices and no longer putting the comfort of the white majority in front of your own.

It's not easy.

Living in the intersection is real and having that reality seen, heard and understood as part of who I am publicly, alongside weaving it into my values and leading with heart has allowed me to walk towards the path of liberation in the way I work and live.

We cannot rely on 'seeing it, to believe it'. We are creating it in real time. And this is revolutionary."[25]

If you are white like me, we have privilege. As such, we do have a responsibility as business owners. As white people we cannot be paralysed by worrying we will do something 'wrong' if we try to address racism in our work and lives.

We need to move past this fear of getting it wrong. In every arena of business, not just allyship. For me the anti-racism work I have done has also prompted me to further my education in what I can do to make my business more LGBTQIA+ inclusive, in small but conscious ways.

If you are a white, cisgender, heterosexual like me, do the work. Educate yourself. Use the resources I've linked to in the index: books, podcasts and courses that already exist to help you understand what you can and should be doing to create both a business, and therefore a society, that is more inclusive and accepting of all.

Because if you're not actively an ally to people who are marginalised, then you are part of the problem. And making a society that is more fair will benefit *everyone*.

And please know that by doing the work the biggest lesson we can take is this: we won't always get it right. Hell, someone reading this may well feel I've not even written this chapter correctly or said enough or used the right words or that I could have used my position here as an author to do more.

My anti-racism and inclusivity work isn't done. I'm not 'fixed'. I am not a perfect role model. I don't and will never fully understand what it's like for someone outside of my skin colour and sexual identity trying to do the things I do with my privilege – build an audience, get speaking engagements, get paying clients.

But it all starts with learning and trying to do *something*. Anything. To change the narrative and make your life and the business you are creating play its part in bringing about a truly equitable world.

Let's recap

1. Your ability to 'just start now' is affected by the privileges you have or don't have in life, no matter how much mindset work you do or actions you take.

2. If you are comparing your path negatively to someone else's, remember that other people's ability to succeed may be reliant on things they are not divulging; you never know the whole picture.

3. If you have privilege, own and acknowledge it and use it as best you can to advocate for others. Be aware that you won't always get it right and that like everything else you do in business, trying your hardest with the best intentions and taking lessons along the way is all part of your growth.

Stop thinking (notice)
> There's something wrong with me
> Why can't I figure this out?
> The world is against me, this will never work

Start thinking (flip to)
> I am enough
> I have the resources I need to succeed
> I am an example of what is possible

8

Your story and words

The most powerful asset any business can have, above and beyond things like a website, a mailing list, a great social media account or fantastic connections is its stories.

Story Coach Rachel Maunder explains:

"Stories bring you and your message to life. They are so much easier for your audience to process, to remember and most importantly to resonate with.

When they hear or read a story, their emotions are engaged. And when their emotions are engaged and aligned with yours, they know that you understand them and are therefore much more likely to want to work with you."[26]

This is backed up by the science of the brain, which Paul J Zak, PhD, speaks about in his book, *The Moral Molecule: How Trust Works*:

> "Stories transmit important information and values from one individual or community to the next. Stories that are personal and emotionally compelling engage more of the brain, and thus are better remembered, than simply stating a set of facts."[27]

If the goal in our marketing is to build 'know, like and trust' factors with our potential customers, stories are going to be crucial to fast-tracking this.

Yet when I say, 'share your story', a whole host of mindset blocks rear their ugly heads and block budding wellness business owners from owning theirs and using them to connect better with their audience (which turns into more customers, more results and more fulfilment).

Let's take the mindsets apart that get in your way when it comes to using your story.

> › I haven't suffered that much, who's going to listen to me?
> › I hate talking about myself, it makes me cringe
> › What will people think of me if I share my story?
> › My life is so boring, what the hell would I share?

I haven't suffered that much, who's going to listen to me?

Top of the list when I help wellness business owners speak up about their own journey is this sort of response:

"I want to help people with endometriosis, but I only ever had mild symptoms, I don't think someone with severe issues is going to listen to me."

Or, "I want to support women with a disordered relationship with food, but I never had a fully blown eating disorder myself. My story's boring really."

"I love helping people who don't know how to cook healthy food, but I've always found it quite easy to do, I don't think I've got a story to tell."

Do any of these resonate with you?

There's absolutely no way I can write a chapter in this book to cover what it takes to own your story without quoting Brené Brown, queen of all things vulnerability.

One of the things Brown teaches in her work and through her *Unlocking Us* podcast is about a concept she calls 'Comparative suffering' which I think is super relevant here. Or the Suffering Olympics as it's also known.

This quote from Brené Brown about Comparative suffering I think perfectly illustrates why these mindsets of 'I haven't suffered enough to share this' are obsolete.

> "Comparative suffering is dangerous. Empathy is not finite. When we practice empathy, we create more empathy.
>
>   Hurt is hurt, and every time we honour our own struggle and the struggles of others by responding with empathy, the healing that results effects all of us."[28]

Your hurt, your experience, your story, no matter how great or small, is valid.

How much you have suffered – or not suffered – with your own health is not the reason that people will choose to invest in you. It might become *part* of the reason. It's just a part of the story your customers connect with.

But in and of itself, it's not the only deciding factor.

Choosing to hide, belittle or diminish your own story because it's not extreme enough, scary enough or life-threatening enough, deprives your potential customers of a chance to connect with you. It prevents that empathy exchange Brown talks about in her definition. And without that empathy, that emotion, people are less likely to buy.

By your logic, if we only listened to people with super extreme stories and experiences when it came to getting help, we'd have a ridiculously small pool of experts to tune into. I'm sure we can all easily identify someone in our sphere with a highly relatable life that we enjoy listening to and learn so much from, but who hasn't had a near-death experience.

Let's take me as an example, as a business owner who wants to inspire you and show you what's possible – but I have absolutely no rags to riches story for you.

I've never been on the breadline. I've never been a single parent. I've never struggled to pay the rent. I've never been in tens of thousands of pounds worth of debt. I know many amazing business coaches that have been in these positions and use this as part of their story to show how incredible their growth and success is.

But I'm not one of them.

Some might say I'm a lacking-in-extremes, slow-growth, chipping-away-with-no-major-story-to-tell, kinda gal.

My story isn't special.

And yet, dear reader, you are still here. You're basically three quarters of the way through my book. My book which I've filled with stories from my own journey to inspire you and show what's possible. Which suggests you feel there's *something* that you can gain from me. Even without a tale of woe or huge upheaval to go alongside it.

In the same way, your story, your journey, no matter what end of the extreme scale it sits on, is valid.

It's more than valid. It helps turn you from just another practitioner into a walking, talking, relatable human being. And people buy from people. Have I mentioned this yet?!

You can still help people even if you haven't been through *exactly* what they have. You need to trust in your tools and abilities. This will come from more and more practice. But it's essential to start with a good solid base of confidence (or courage, as Brené Brown would say), to show up and own your experience and expertise. Go back to Chapter 3 if you need to revisit the idea of your value and worth without the need to learn more or have gone through more.

I hate talking about myself, it makes me cringe

Okay, buckle up. This is a big one. And it requires a total reframe of why I encourage you to share your stories in whatever way you can.

Talking about your journey isn't about you.

Sharing your experiences isn't to make you look better.

Opening up and being vulnerable about what you've been through isn't to make you appear a better prospect.

It's to help your ideal customer.

We need to remove your ego from this.

And I use 'ego' in the kindest, most compassionate way I can. I use 'ego' in the same way that Eckhart Tolle does in his books, such as *The Power Of Now*. To describe the over-thinking, over-analysing, worrying, socially-conditioned brain powered 'you' that you've come to think of as yourself.

That's not actually you. It's just a series of thought patterns and habits and societal messages. The real *you* isn't ego. We need to remove your ego from this. And connect with the real you.

When we remove the ego we come back to one simple fact: what you are trying to do when you market your wellness business is help people.

The best way you can help people is to communicate as effectively as possible why someone should jump on board and invest in working with you.

It's literally your job to be clear about how you help and use the most efficient methods possible to promote action in your audience. Because action (for your ideal client that means investment in you) = results for them. Otherwise, you are leaving people ruminating, contemplating and procrastinating, still stuck in their lives and symptoms that are bringing them down and holding them back.

Sharing your story is the most helpful thing you can do.

If you're still shrinking from the idea of sharing your narrative, let me throw some research at you.

Throwing research at people won't make them buy.

Reeling off scientific data does very little to convince anyone of their need for your service. If you're thinking, "No one needs to hear my story, I'll just hit them with the facts", then you are mistaken.

Telling your audience the big stats about their health conditions or the numbers that surround your solution in actual fact could do more to hinder someone investing in you than it does help them.

On the flip side, if we can personalise, humanise, and tell one single story about how what you do has an effect, this helps prospective customers connect, relate, and feel ready to buy.

Talking about your journey isn't about you. It's to help your ideal customer.

Bombarding people with big headlines, general facts, the vague problems you tackle and outcomes you help achieve doesn't drive people to buy.

Storytelling and bringing things back to a single human story or journey is what enables people to really connect with what you do and relate it to themselves, so they are moved to take action.

If this is still all feeling a bit too uncomfortable to talk about yourself, then I would recommend that you start using your clients and the people you help as the examples you centre your stories on. With full permission or anonymously, whatever works for you and them. But the crucial part is the storytelling needs to be there. Not just the facts.

What will people think of me if I share my story?

If I had to pick the most common issue I see new wellness practitioners face that totally blocks their ability to share what they do, it's fear of judgement. And this doesn't just apply to sharing your story. It spreads its nasty cold fingers over all aspects of our businesses if we're scared of what other people think.

> What will my social media followers think if I charge that?
> What will my colleagues at work say if I post that video?

> What will my mum/sister/auntie do if I tell them I'm turning this into a job?

It's all variations on a theme but it all comes back to one thing: fear of being judged.

We need to dismantle this permanently.

Firstly, it's important to really dig in and logically look at the facts. Sometimes our good old friend the inner critic is telling us that *all these people* are judging us.

But are they?

Who are *all the people?*

Are we dealing with a fear of strangers on the Internet or specific named people who are known to you?

Let's take the strangers first. I'm hoping, now I've phrased it like that – strangers – that you're already getting the reminder that this is a group of people that you don't know, and who don't know you.

You don't know them – or know whether they're a nice, helpful, friendly, kind, well-informed, well-meaning person, or that perhaps they're not. And they don't know you – that you're a hard-working, well-intentioned, highly-educated and nuanced person. In which case . . . do you really care about their opinions?

Are you going to let total strangers on the Internet that do not know you at all, stop you from telling your story and doing what you're trained to do?

Can you hear how absurd that sounds?!

I hope our logic here is smashing your mindset block into tiny, irreparable pieces right now on this one!

But if there is still a quiet but powerful voice in your head that's saying, "Yes Vicky, I think I am going to let them stop me, I'm still scared", then I urge you to try this hack. Write a list of the people whose opinions actually matter to you.

Your list will probably be a small handful of people. I know mine are my husband, my mentor, a few family members and a couple of very close business buddies who know me well and have my back.

Beyond that, no one else has the full picture and understanding of who I am and what I'm trying to achieve, nor do I look up to anyone else for advice. Anyone outside of that inner circle I have created for myself can't have an opinion so strong and well informed that it would stop me doing what I want to do.

What is it they say? If you wouldn't take advice from them, don't take criticism from them.

Strangers on the Internet – do your worst judging. But you're not stopping me.

However.

Sometimes it's not 'the people' out there on the Internet.

What if it *is* specific people that you know that you're afraid of judgement from?

If that's you, I hear you.

Maybe it's your old boss, your mum, your flatmate, or your boyfriend's parents. You can see their face, you've interpreted that raised eyebrow when you talk about your work, you can imagine the words coming out of their mouth. You play out conversations with them in your head where they point out all the things you're doing wrong or that are making you look foolish.

If you have a name, a face, then firstly tell me this: is this person definitely judging you? Has something judgemental or unhelpful actually come out of their mouth to date?

Or is it all a total fabrication your crafty inner critic has come up with as yet *another* way to sabotage you being visible and sharing what you want with the world?

I asked my client Samantha this question once when we were discussing her fear of judgement from her flatmate. As we analysed the real-life interactions she'd had with her flatmate (not the fictional ones in her head), Samantha came to realise that her flatmate had always been incredibly supportive, interested in her work and keen to hear more. Not judgemental and disapproving, as it had turned into in her mind when she played it out.

Like Samantha, I'd like to hazard a guess that of the 90% of the people you *think* are judging you, most probably aren't.

In fact, when we talk to people we know about what we do, they're usually extremely encouraging and positive. They ask questions and want the best for us. They're usually the opposite of judgemental. We're just too afraid to let them in sometimes or have those honest conversations with them.

Of course, though, that might not always be the case.

If the people that you have identified are *honestly* judging you and have negative opinions about what you are doing and sharing and they've made it clear to you already, then know this: their judgement and opinions say far more about *them*, than it does about *you*.

Their words and thoughts might reflect:

> Their own deep insecurities about being visible and putting themselves out there
> Their own limiting beliefs and mindsets about what it means to run a business
> Their own missed opportunities and life choices which they feel are triggered when they see you taking action

None of these things bear any relation to you and whether what you are doing is good or bad. If they have a negative opinion, then that doesn't mean you've got it wrong.

You and your life and business are totally separate from them and their issues.

Remember we were talking about taking the ego out of things, and focusing on the people you're trying to help? It's the same principle here. You need to remove the people who are judging and bringing you down and replace them in your thoughts with the ideal customer for what you are offering.

Sometimes this will just be removing them from your mind and your every day thoughts by addressing how you're thinking. Sometimes this might look like more boundaries and distance in a physical sense. Only you will know what is needed to ensure you keep yourself in a great head space.

Because the people who don't like the way you're doing things?

They're not your ideal customer.

If you're looking to set up a wellness business that helps people with their health, your 100% focus should be on the potential customers for your services and offers, their wants and needs and problems. Not on people who will never buy from you or benefit from all your amazing knowledge and expertise.

We do have to have slightly Teflon exterior if we're running our own business and putting ourselves out there. It comes with the territory that marketing yourself does mean the possibility of some people not liking you, whether they're known to you or not.

The more your audience grows, the more chance there is statistically that someone will see you and decide you are not their cup of tea (just like the man who watched me dancing in my Instagram video and decided he thought I was an overeater).

I've touched already in Chapter 4 on the feeling of pressure to 'get it right' and the fear of being judged by your professional peers. And in Chapter 7 we looked at privilege and the fact that for some of us, just the sheer act being visible may well result in being judged and commented on, simply for being ourselves.

The cold hard truth is this. Not everyone is going to like who you are, what you do, and the way you do things.

I used to run a series of women's wellness retreats and

our events varied from five-night breaks on the Algarve in Portugal, to brunch mornings creating vision boards. After all our events I was fastidious about collecting feedback to get a sense of what people had enjoyed and how we could improve.

Largely the feedback was positive – a few constructive criticisms but all things we could incorporate into our next events.

But occasionally the feedback was harsh. After one vision board brunch with largely positive praise and appreciation from the 30 plus attendees, one participant (who interestingly chose to remain nameless) slammed the whole event in her feedback survey.

What did you think of the timings? Badly managed.

What did you think of the materials included? Rubbish.

What did you think of the venue and the food? Poor.

Would you attend one of our other events? No.

Wow. We always had to take these occasional negative bits of feedback with a pinch of salt and always within the context of the other feedback we'd received. Not everyone was going to like and appreciate what we did.

When Instagram started offering their Reels feature (short videos, I mentioned in Chapter 7, which many use to dance, lip-sync or make people laugh) I jumped at the chance to use them to show a different side to my personality.

But the more I did, the more followers I *lost*.

Yup, that's right – for all the online marketing advice that was circulating at the time that said, "Reels are the best way to grow your audience fast right now!" I was actually *losing* people in mine. Which meant that people who previously had thought they would like and gain from my content,were turned off by the way I showed who I was through these short video clips.

Now I could have taken that to mean I should stop producing Reels. And go back to what I was doing before, without the funny, light-hearted, sketch-style interludes.

But I didn't. I kept going. Why? Because I love making them! They're fun, they allow me to be silly and creative and for the right people, *my* people, they create a deeper understanding of what I'm like as a human, beyond the helpful (but serious) tips.

It's okay to not be everyone's cup of tea. In fact, if my examples are anything to go by, it's a sign that you're standing out, getting noticed and that your opinions and style are unique. It's a sign that you're in the arena (as Brené Brown would say) – that you're giving it a go, that you put something out there and that you tried your best to help and serve.

All of these signs give you a much greater chance of attracting the people who *do* want to work with you. The ones that get you and want more from you. And those are ultimately the only people you should be focusing on.

Don't shy away from repelling the people that aren't right for you. I know it feels alien to go into something knowing a potential outcome is to not be liked. But it's worth it if your real people are drawn in in the process.

When does sharing become oversharing?

This is a question I get asked a lot.

You want to share your stories and you see that human connection and authenticity is valued and results in increased trust. But when does that tip over into gratuitous sharing that's verging on voyeurism?

How much do you have to open up and be totally *seen* in order to get people to buy from you? And when does sharing and baring all actually become a turn off for potential customers?

I've seen both extremes.

I once had a client who was doing all the right things when it came to creating content for her business. She was clear on who she helped, she was writing copy that related to their situation, talking through their blocks and selling her offers.

At a logical, practical level, all the pieces were there.

But . . . her content lacked soul. It lacked personality. It lacked . . . her.

She never showed up on live video on her social media. Any photos of herself she shared were always her professional headshots, full make-up, formal-looking outfits and hair straightened. There were no personal anecdotes or insights into her, the full human being behind the shiny-haired photos, stock images and carefully written captions.

There was a part of herself that she didn't want to reveal. That kept her hidden. And as a result, whilst her offers sold, there was never the ease and flow and authenticity that I believe should come with great business. It was hard work. She wasn't being her full self. And that's what people want.

Your audience can read between the lines and tell when you're not being your whole self. We're so incredibly perceptive as humans. Even a sniff of deception or suppression of truth, and we get the sense we can't fully trust this person. And without the trust? The sales don't come.

At the other end of the spectrum, whilst I've never helped someone directly like this myself (most of my clients are at the 'I'm too scared to share anything' stage!), my sister once told me she followed of a cake-baking business owner who would regularly have panic attacks in her own shop and would lock herself into a store cupboard at the back of the premises and livestream the experience on her social media.

That's more like car-crash TV to me. And not exactly conducive with building a relationship with your audience where you're viewed as someone who carries some level of authority and responsibility, which is what comes when someone is looking to invest in you.

I also don't advocate 'you okay hun?' style content sharing. What I mean by this is deliberately fishing for engagement and connection by posting a half story or emotional plea or attention seeking cry for help or reassurance. "We're in the hospital, please think of me", but no further context. No thanks. Not for me. That's not transparency.

According to the Deloitte Trust Drives Profitable Pricing research[29], trust is based on four factors: humanity, transparency, capability and reliability. Coming across as someone who is less than reliable or transparent can erode that trust.

So how do you get the balance?

As with everything else in your business (hello Chapter 4!) – it's about experimenting. Giving it a go. Seeing what feels good. Pushing the boundaries, a little more each week. Watching others and trying out what they're doing to see if it's a good fit for you.

Noticing, observing and gently challenging the thoughts and barriers your mind puts in your way. "I can't share that picture of me from my walk with the dog, I didn't have any make-up on", for example. Is that really true? What would happen if you did?

I can't possibly give you a hard-and-fast list of share this but don't share this. It's so individual. The only way you're going to find that balance for you is to give it a go. You can't say you don't like it until you've tried it.

My life is so boring, what the hell would I share?

One of the most common rebuffs I get when I encourage clients to share their story or their day-to-day life for nuggets of wisdom is this. My life is so boring, who would want to watch it?

Do you know who?

Your ideal client.

Remember the sliding scale I introduced you to in Chapter 3? The image where you're a few steps ahead of where your dream customer is right now? The things you think are mundane and are part of your everyday life are the bits people want to tune into and learn from.

The way you put that lunch bowl together, that's something they can't do.

Your ability to get your 10,000 steps in effortlessly, that's something they haven't figured out. The mindset you adopt when faced with your micro-managing boss, they wish they had that.

If you show them, demonstrate to them and *live* the life they want – whether that's just a couple, or many steps ahead of where they are, they can more quickly see how you can help them. They can see that you're doing it yourself. Or you're enabling other people in the same way *they* want to be enabled.

The reality is much of my own business is that it involves sitting behind a laptop typing or talking. I could decide that I'm extremely dull based on that analysis and therefore share nothing with my audience, because who wants to just watch me at a computer all day?

But I don't. Instead, I pick out elements of my day to reveal, like my to-do list, a presentation I'm putting together, some thoughts after a client session or a podcast I'm enjoying. I disclose them in the full trust that my ideal customer *will* find it fascinating to get a behind-the-scenes look at what I get up to. I even share my lunches and recipe-testing dinners and am told it inspires other business owners to eat better and give new food a go!

If people find it boring, they don't have to stick around! But by sharing how I live my life it moves everything I teach from just the theory to a real-life example my ideal customers can relate to. They can imagine being in my space, talking to me, getting my advice and guidance. Because I've shown them and helped them connect via storytelling.

Do you definitely need stories?

Am I saying that it's impossible to have a business that thrives and share zero personal stories? No, I'm not. There are millions of ways to make money and sell your stuff. There's not a fixed, 'right' way. You do you.

But for most solopreneur wellness practitioners, given *you* are the human that they're booking to work with, sharing stories is a great way to build trust with potential clients. And it shouldn't be as scary as you've made it out to be.

I'm hoping that I've expressed convincingly throughout this chapter that storytelling, vulnerability and opening up to human-to-human connection is going to fast-track the trust that people need to have in you to be ready to invest. It also makes doing business and showing up to market yourself and connect with people *so* much easier if you are being your true self.

Let's recap

1. Storytelling, vulnerability and opening up to human-to-human connection is going to fast-track the trust that people need to have in you to be ready to invest.

2. People probably aren't judging you as much as you think they are. If they are, that says more about them than it does about you. Plus, they're not your ideal customer, and your ideal customer is the only person you really should be focusing on.

3. The only way to strike the balance between under and oversharing is to give it a go.

4. Your life isn't boring, there are so many lessons your audience can learn from it, way more than just the theory. Demonstrating how you live the day-to-day can inspire people and help them imagine working with you.

Stop thinking (notice)

> Who's going to listen to me?
> What will people think of me?
> Who am I to say this?

Start thinking (flip to)

> I can inspire people every day
> My voice is needed
> Who am I *not* to share this?

9

Running out of time and staying motivated

To me, connection is all about finding the people who are going to buy from you – and others along the way that will help and lift you up.

It's all the buzz words you hear: community, audience, followers, subscribers, fans, evangelists. Without them, you don't have a business.

But building an audience, a customer base for what you're offering, takes time.

People buy from providers they know, like and trust.

They can get to know you and make a decision about liking you fairly quickly. Perhaps in just one encounter – if they watch a video or hear you on a podcast interview or stumble across your social media where you are saying *exactly* what they need to hear.

But the trust?

Trust takes time.

I mentioned the Deloitte Trust Drives Profitable Pricing research from 2021 in Chapter 8. In that same study of over 100,000 people, Deloitte found that "62% of customers buy almost exclusively from *trusted* brands and 88% of customers who *highly trust* a brand have bought from the brand again."

> Trust is the foundation of the human experience; it is impossible to build successful relationships without it.[30]

Selling and communicating is all about relationships. People buy from people. It's something I've mentioned a couple of times already through the course of this book. Human experience is essential to getting someone ready to invest in you. It's not your shiny logo or your excellent long list of credentials they're looking at. It's you, the person that they trust.

Building trust doesn't happen overnight. Yes, there are clever ways to fast-track the process, to help people get to know, like and trust you more quickly than they might otherwise. That's basically what effective marketing is.

But a really solid, ethical business is built with consistency, over time.

The vast majority of people who buy from you are those who have known and seen your content and your reliability for an extended period. But I know time is something we all feel short on.

I'm running out of time

In Chapter 1, I told you how important it is to take time to set goals. In Chapter 2 I told you that we need to eliminate "I don't have time" from our vocabulary. In Chapter 4 we talked about how nothing in your business is a waste of time. And here I am again talking about your time.

That's because for me this is one of the biggest and most consistent blocks that business owners face when they are just starting out and so I wanted to do a deeper dive into it and the ways that you can reframe your mindset around time.

Because yes, I am not mistaken. I genuinely see lack of time as a mindset issue, not a calendar issue.

Let me explain.

Because I see you. I know you're secretly still reading this book (we're almost at the end!) and thinking, "Yeah yeah, I get it, Vicky, it takes time. But it'll be different for me!"

You're here for the fast-acting tips and quick wins. That's where you're at. You're done with fannying around and want to see some results now from all your hard work. Or maybe you don't want to entertain things taking a long time if you're right at the start of your business building journey.

You've already put so much into this – your qualification alone has taken a huge amount of money and hours, perhaps even years of your life.

Time is of the essence now. You want to see some tangible results from all the work you're putting in.

I hear you.

Those pressures are real. They're pressing. If you want to turn this into full-time income, you don't want to be experimenting and learning for years. It needs to turn a profit – and soon.

This is the honest reality of staying alive and paying the bills in the modern world. If you've quit all other income sources to pursue this, I'm not going to pretend that that sort of time pressure doesn't exist. You can't live on experience and fresh air. I get it.

But the problem with thinking you're running out of time and that you *need* to make this work is that it totally and utterly strangles the fun, lightness, playfulness, enjoyment, creativity and experimentation that is *absolutely necessary* for your business to flourish.

And without that fun and lightness, you know what those 'I'm running out of time' vibes reek of?

Desperation.

And I can assure you, ain't no customer ever bought because of your desperation to make a sale.

People buy because they see your passion, your excitement and your *positivity* that you can help them. They see the ease with which you do things. They don't buy because you're so anxious to make money and get clients that you'll say or do anything.

How do we reframe our approach to time to allow in that ease?

The way I see it, there's two ways of looking at time:

1. Life is short. Go do that thing.
2. You have all the time in the world. Relax, it's all coming to you.

I think sometimes we do need a little push to get on with things. Life isn't forever. We only get a short time on this planet. Some shorter than others, sadly.

Personally, my kick up the backside when I'm procrastinating is to remember those who *don't* have the opportunity to even make 'wrong' decisions anymore, or to dabble in experimenting.

I had a friend, Caroline, who inspired me to leave my job back when I was toying with the idea of starting my own business. We met through Instagram, both sharing recipes and food photography. I learned that Caroline had courageously left her high-earning, high-powered, jet-setting corporate job to retrain as a Nutritional Therapist. If she can do it, so can I, I thought. I handed my notice in a week after meeting her in person for lunch.

But as we both began to navigate earning for ourselves, building online audiences and turning ourselves into business owners with limitless earning potential and a dream life ahead of us doing what we loved, something awful happened.

Caroline was diagnosed with stage 4 cancer. And despite an incredible fight, she did run out of time. At age 35 she passed away, leaving behind a husband, toddler son and her dreams of becoming a Nutritional Therapist.

So when I'm fannying around worrying about what the 'right' thing is to launch next, or how awful it will be to make the 'wrong' decision about what to post on social media or how to pitch myself for a speaking event, or staring into my bank account wishing it was a bit bigger – I remember what an incredible privilege it is to even have the option to make a decision and get it 'right' or 'wrong'. Some people don't get that chance.

(Incidentally when Caroline knew she didn't have much time left, she fast-tracked her desire to write a cookbook. And through the amazing collaborative power of social media, she had the recipes tested, photographed and the book self-published before she passed away. Sometimes when you know you don't have much time, you get things done).

However. Motivating ourselves from a place of fear or lack *constantly* isn't helpful either. I'm certainly not wishing stage 4 cancer on any of you to motivate you to take action. Whilst our own mortality is something helpful to reflect on when we need that little jolt into action, mostly I find it more freeing to spend 95% of my waking and working hours thinking and believing that I *do* have time. And that actually I am:

1. Right where I am meant to be in this moment
2. Learning the lessons I need from the situation I find myself in
3. In full trust that everything I desire (money, clients, reputation) is coming to me
4. Laying the foundations for everything I want

Changing your mindset and that story that there isn't enough time into a more empowering statement from the list above (or anything else that makes you feel like you *do* have time on your side), is vital to bring in the ease and flow of successful business. Rather than feeling we're pushing, forcing, and strangling our fledgling business into making it work for us.

Feeling motivated

The word motivation has popped up a few times now as we've discussed the topic of time and so I wanted to address it as it's something I get asked about a lot.

"I've set myself goals and I do really want to achieve them, and I know my big 'why'", said a voice note from my client Disha one day, "but sometimes I just really lack motivation to take action and do all the things I've set myself. Is that normal?"

Does that sound familiar?

There are lots of classic hacks to keep yourself motivated.

> Set clear goals
> Break down your goals into manageable tasks
> Be held accountable by a mentor or a friend
> Stop multitasking and distracting yourself
> Keep it fun and reward yourself when you achieve your goals

These tools absolutely do work. I employ a lot of them myself – both in my own work and for others in the communities I create for new business owners.

But honestly? I don't believe even with all the tools in the world you will *always* feel motivated. Not in that preppy, pumped up, run to your desk, buzzing with excitement kind of way. Not every single day.

You're a human being, not a robot. You will have good days and bad days, hormonal days, days where there's other stuff that takes priority, days where things just feel hard.

The answer to Disha's question is absolutely yes, it's normal to not feel motivated all the time.

There is nothing wrong with you if there are hours, days or weeks where you don't feel 'motivated' in the classic sense.

There have been many, many moments in my business, and even in writing this book, where I have not felt motivated. This chapter for example has been a bit like pulling teeth if I'm honest.

If I went into the book writing process expecting to feel excited and motivated every single day I showed up to add words to the page, I'd never have got the thing done.

Instead, I acknowledge that some days it feels great and fun, and other days it feels hard and like it's all a bit pointless.

But I keep going. I keep showing up.

I think one of the most helpful metaphors I've come across for this ebb and flow of work and motivation

Some days it feels
great and fun, other
days it feels
hard and like
it's pointless.
Keep going.
Keep showing up.

came from business coach Jen Carrington when she described work in seasons.[31]

> Seasons of hustle (when things are going well, you're on a roll, people are buying, you're in the zone)
> Seasons of struggle (things feel difficult, people aren't buying, nothing flows, you're questioning everything)
> Seasons of rest (holidays, quiet, reflection, working 'on' and not 'in' your business)

When I see my work and life in these patterns, I can be more compassionate to myself. To see that it's just a phase and that those great moments of flow will return. To know that I just need to ride the wave and accept and find peace in whatever season I'm in at the time.

Once again, being in any of these seasons is just a sign that I'm *doing the work*. Which is a surefire way of knowing that I'm getting somewhere, even if I don't always feel motivated.

I'm just a bit lazy

When I first started my healthy eating food blog I wrote out a plan of what recipes I wanted to create. Currently a blank website, I wanted to populate the blog with a balanced mix of different meal types.

To get me started I wrote out lists of breakfast, snacks, lunch, dinners and sweet treats ideas I had. I formulated a plan and broke it down (following all the motivation tactics). Each Monday I'd post the next recipe on the planner, giving myself the week to test and the weekend to finalise and photograph the finished dish.

I remember so vividly sitting on my bed in my little one-bed flat in London, writing this plan and filling it with 15 to 20 weeks' worth of content.

The plan looked amazing. Loads of recipes I was excited to create and share.

So, what did I do after I'd written all that out?

Did I feel super motivated by my plan?

Did I hop to it and get into the kitchen to start baking?

Nope!

Honestly? I closed the laptop and I didn't look at that plan, or the blog, for another few weeks.

I had the plan. I'd started the website. I had the time. (I was in a long-distance relationship, living alone and all my friend were married and starting to have kids, I didn't have exactly a hopping social schedule!)

Yet the blog that I was all passionate and excited about was sat there empty.

Was this . . . laziness?

Would you say that I was being lazy in this situation?

Because this is the exact situation I see lots of my clients in. Having a plan, having time, having done some of the work and yet . . . never quite seeing it all through to the end.

I want to make sure you know, just like me with my blog, you are 100% not lazy if this is where you find yourself.

And I know that because look at what you've done.

You've trained and worked so hard to get your qualification. There was a clear structure, a framework and regular feedback within the college or institution you trained with to keep you motivated and moving forwards. You have proved to yourself over and over through doing that (and no doubt lots of other achievements in your life) that you are anything but lazy. You can and have achieved great things before.

But this is different.

Working for yourself (or *trying* to work for yourself, whilst in reality feeling like you're messing around and achieving nothing when you first start) doesn't have that structure. Unless you join a programme or get some coaching support.

There isn't a boss.

And yes, that's *great* in lots of ways; it's a big driver for so many of us to be without the demands and deadlines and beck-and-call of an employer. I've lost count of the times I've been told on coaching calls, "I am a terrible employee, I'm born to be an entrepreneur!"

But there are downsides to losing that structure too.

No deadlines. No praise. No feedback. No sage wisdom. No relaxing because someone else can help pick up the pieces if it doesn't work out. No pay packet at the end of the month, regardless of your output.

If you're not taking action in your business, it's not because you're lazy. I promise.

"I'm lazy" is just another way to say "I don't have time."

And they both have a hidden meaning.

People who say "I don't have time" busy themselves with feeling productive and taking *other* actions, but not doing the things that will move the needle.

People who say "I'm just lazy" know that they have time available, but willingly fill it with escape mechanisms and distractions, instead of doing the things that will move the needle.

What they both really mean through their words and actions is:

> I don't know how to do it
> I'm afraid of failure
> I'm afraid of what happens if it *does* work out (otherwise known as fear of success)
> I don't want to be visible
> I'm afraid of judgement
> I'd rather stay in my comfort zone

If we're going to stop saying "I don't have time" then I'd encourage you to also ditch "I'm lazy" from your vocabulary.

I wasn't being lazy when I didn't get cracking on my food blog straightaway. I felt overwhelmed with the work I'd given myself.

There were a lot of things I didn't know how to do – the food photography was all new to me, I hated baking so some of the sweet recipes I'd planned were probably going to take more time than I had anticipated.

I was also spending a lot of time on Instagram following incredible recipe developers and food photographers who were streets ahead of where I was in terms of skills and knowledge. What would they think of my rubbish cooking and pictures?

So rather than laziness, it was a checklist of both "I don't know how" and "I'm afraid of judgement", all underlined with "I'd rather stay in my comfort zone" (good old inner critic keeping me safe).

When I realised this, I tweaked the plan.

I moved to a fortnightly posting schedule – I was still working a full-time job after all. I saved a lot of other great food photos that I admired so that when I came to take my own, I had similar layouts and concepts I could follow. And I spent more time on my social media revisiting the other 'little guys' accounts like mine, beginner foodies just sharing the recipes they loved without fancy props or DSLR cameras to help boost my confidence that I had something to offer.

I got my blog started of course. And it went on to win two awards while it was live. And all the work and moments of both high and low motivation brought me here today, writing this.

I'm glad I kept powering through. I had the time and I'm not lazy. The same goes for you and where your business can take you if you just start now.

Let's recap

1. Building a solid business based in trust takes time. There aren't any shortcuts that are sustainable. Embrace the journey.

2. Needing your business to work quickly reeks of desperation, which is one of the most unattractive states you can be in when trying to build relationships with prospective customers.

3. We all have a limited amount of time on this planet. More likely you'll regret what you don't try than what you do.

4. Motivation comes and goes. There are ways to hack it, but it's also important to understand there's nothing wrong with you if some days (or weeks) feel stickier than others.

5. You're not lazy. More likely you're afraid or don't know what to do. Be kind to yourself and notice the *real* stories that are stopping you from taking action.

Stop thinking (notice)

> This *needs* to work and make money soon
> I'm running out of time
> I'm lazy

Start thinking (flip to)

> Work comes in seasons, I accept the season I am in right now
> I never regret taking action and giving it a try
> What's worth having takes time to build

10

Showing up even if it feels like no one is listening

When I take people through the core content of getting their wellness business set up, I save the 'finding clients' section until last.

This is often the missing piece of the jigsaw that clicks everything into place. We've laid all the foundations, got all the structures and systems set up, created products ready to buy and worked on your mindset around selling and being of service . . . now it's time to go out and connect with the people that need you.

When you first start doing this it looks like:

> Writing emails
> Posting on social media
> Going to networking events

> Pitching yourself as a guest speaker
> Sending out emails to a mailing list

The list of course, goes on.

These tasks take up a lot of your time. I know, I've been there.

I've spent days writing emails, going to events and creating content for social media in order to attract in an audience.

And in the early days, I'll be honest . . . I got very little back.

Days turn into weeks and it honestly felt like I was talking to absolutely no one.

You get a couple of token gesture 'likes' on your social media posts. You might see a trickle of people hitting your website when you check the analytics, but no enquiries. You have some interesting conversations at networking events but nothing that's going to turn into a customer straightaway.

Sometimes it feels like for all your effort, you're attracting totally the wrong people. The only people that seem to pay any attention to your social media posts are your peers – your college buddies who want to see what you're doing or other practitioners nosing around your website and accounts.

Or, heaven help you, it's just predatory business coaches dropping into your inbox telling you they can fix everything for you, rather than genuine punters who need your help.

That voice in your head is starting to get louder: "What the hell are you doing? You're spending so much time on this. Are you actually reaching anyone at all that is going to buy from you?"

This is the point at which your inner critic will be having an absolute field day. It's got all the evidence in the tumbleweed to tell you loudly and repeatedly that you are a total failure and this is never going to work.

In all honesty, this was my reality for many weeks and months when I started my business. I would be in tears on a regular basis with my husband, asking for reassurances that it would all work out, because yet another week had passed where no one was buying. Those inner critics shouts in my head were so loud sometimes it was like being followed around by a school bully that wouldn't leave me alone.

> ❯ What do you think you're doing sat at that laptop all day?
> ❯ This isn't a *real* job, you don't know what you're doing.
> ❯ No one's listening, no one's buying. Just give up.
> ❯ You're a failure. This is never going to work.

But none of this was true.

That quiet, that wait, that gap as you keep showing up: that's normal.

It's not your fault that you think you're failing if this silence happens to you as well. There are two main culprits we can point the finger at instead:

The Instant Gratification problem

One of the big issues with the modern marketing field today, and in particular social media, is that it's based on instant gratification.

We are primed to post content and take action based solely on whether it gets a reaction from people straight-away. Likes, comments, saves, shares. The elusive 'going viral'. We post and keep checking our phones to get that mini dopamine hit to tell us we're hitting the mark and getting it 'right'.

Because of the way these platforms are designed we start to believe that if we don't get a great reaction instantly that we're not cut out for this. That if people don't like, share, enquire and book straightaway, they never will.

I promise they will. But it's a conscious effort to train your mind to keep thinking and believing this, when all the tools we use imply that we've failed if we don't see instant success.

The truth is it's necessary for you to keep taking action, and doing things that are for you and your business's long term benefit, *even if you don't see an instant reaction.*

If you're doing the strategic things, they'll pay dividends down the line, even if in the moment they feel like they're having no effect because you don't get a response straightaway.

One example is writing blog posts. As someone who's built an audience and cut their teeth on all things audience building online through a healthy eating food blog, I'm a massive advocate of blogging for your business as a truly sustainable way to get found, get enquiries and make income.

And yet I can't tell you how hard it is for me to convince clients that it's a better use of their time to write a blog post that will exist on their website and get them found years into the future, instead of posting something to social media in the here and now.

"But Vicky! No one reads my blog! I'm barely getting any website traffic! It's pointless! If I post a little something on my Instagram I might get ten likes right now though . . . And that makes me feel good and loved. I'll do that instead."

Instant. Gratification.

It's not just marketing that suffers the curse of instant gratification, it's a problem for modern life as a whole. Think about it in another sphere of life: health.

When it comes to their health, people want quick wins and big results with limited input and minimal chance of failure. I've no doubt you battle on a daily basis seeing people in your audience who want fast change, rather than valuing long-lasting, slow and sustainable adjustments that can genuinely change their life.

It's the same for business growth.

If you want a life-changing business you have to be prepared to do things slowly and sustainably to get that kind of impact. You won't see results overnight.

The fallacy of overnight success

Why do most people think they must be failing if things are all quiet on the western front?

Because we've all been sold a lie.

I don't want to keep going on about it as I've raised it already, quite a few times. But just to reiterate as we draw to the close of this book that it is *not* normal or possible for 99% of people to launch a business and be fully booked within weeks.

If you are being fed this message by anyone in your life – be it online or offline – I suggest you step away and reassess where you're getting your business advice from and if it's promoting an ethical and realistic way to grow and get clients.

Business models that get quick results are often based on huge investments, shady tactics, pushing people that aren't suitable into a sale, and constant launch cycles that are stressful – and inconsistent with enjoyable and sustainable business growth.

In my eyes, if you aren't seeing instant results that's something to look on as a good thing. And that flies in the face of a lot of what we're told. But I really believe you'll learn far more and have a greater basis of trust with your audience if you grow and get clients over a longer period of time, which will involve a slow and quiet start to your journey.

The compound effect

What this all comes down to is that it's never about one thing.

It's not about how many people reply to your email the day you sent it. Or book you immediately after seeing you speak at an event. Or comment on your social media post in the first 30 minutes it goes live.

It's never about a single action. Or a single result.

It's about the compound effect. It's what happens when you add up all the tiny steps you take and the messages you put out there, even if it feels like no one is hearing you.

And it's an age-old approach.

Within marketing spheres, for nearly 100 years, there has been a philosophy that people need to see your content at least seven times before they'll buy: it's a marketing maxim developed by the movie industry in the 1930s. Back then, studio bigwigs discovered that a certain amount of repeat promotion was required in order to see the box office sales they wanted.

Even 100 years ago marketing experts knew that putting up a single poster was not going to make their film a sold out sensation. So why would we be able to fast-track that now?

In fact, it's the opposite. In the wake of the modern era and the technology now at our disposal, that number of times that people need to see you before they're ready to buy has *increased* exponentially, not decreased. People need to see you *far* more times than seven to be ready to

It's never about
a single action.

Or a single result.

It's about the
compound effect.

buy, simply because of the sheer amount of information they sift through on a daily basis.

And it's not just any old seven things. Your audience needs to see good quality, impactful content to move them to invest. Not just relentless sales pitches.

So with all that in mind, you'll be talking and putting out content for a lot of your working hours as a business owner. And it will feel for quite a considerable time as if you are talking to yourself.

But I promise you, you aren't.

It is all adding up.

Even if right now, in this moment, it doesn't feel like it.

Keep repeating yourself

One of the big blockers I find wellness practitioners face when it comes to creating content consistently is the worry that they're repeating themselves.

> I've already covered this topic before, I don't want to bore people
> I wrote a blog about this six months ago, why would I share it again?
> I put all these tips in a video I made last week, what should I share now?

It is a big joke in my family that I hate repetition. My Dad and stepmum once had a wonderful holiday in the idyllic village of Southwold, Suffolk, in the UK. They referred to it so many times in stories at the dinner table that I eventually snapped, "Yes I know! You've told us this before!" It's become a running joke that I can't stand to listen to repeated tales so they now mention that trip and the word 'Southwold' in mock hushed tones when they want to talk about it around me.

But marketing is totally different.

As much as in my own life I'm at great pains to say, "I can't remember if I've told you this before so stop me if I have . . ." when I tell a story to my family, in my business I will *never* apologise for being repetitive. I know it's necessary to convert people into buyers.

News flash. You will be repeating yourself a lot when it comes to what content you create and publish.

And that's actually a good thing.

Repeating yourself (by which I mean talking about the same thing but in lots of different ways, not saying the *exact* same thing because that would be boring) means:

> Your audience see you as a consistent, reliable source of information – elevating your authority position
> You're more likely to be seen saying what's needed by the people that might have missed what you shared elsewhere or in weeks gone by
> You're giving yourself far more opportunities to hit on the exact language and delivery that really clicks for an prospective customer and gets them ready to buy

Keep repeating yourself. It works.

The magic of the Law of Attraction when you're busy talking to no one

The other exciting outcome I discovered from taking action and riding the wave of the compound effect – even when it felt like talking into an abyss – is that sometimes there are unexpected, positive outcomes.

When I joined a membership back in the early days of my business to learn how to build my online audience (after a good few months struggling by myself to figure it out and eventually conceding I needed help) there was a simple recommendation above and beyond any clever social media or mailing list strategies. Write to five people personally, directly, every single day that could buy from you or help you.

So I stuck to this rule. Before I allowed myself to do anything else in my business, each day I would sit down and write five emails to people in my network to tell them about what I was offering and asking if they'd like to buy it.

To start with it felt really cringy. Pushy even. And wow . . . doing it every day? To five people? Over and over? It was definitely out of my comfort zone.

My inner critic was screaming to stay small and just hide behind writing a few more blogs or posting on social media.

But I stuck with it. And I started to notice something amazing happening.

I'd start the morning with writing those five emails. And would those five people reply? No, not usually. Certainly not immediately. Sometimes they never replied at all, even after days or weeks! But what did happen? Other things came in.

Buyers I didn't know about purchased. Opportunities I didn't expect popped up. People signed up to my mailing list. There was growth in other areas.

I mentioned the Law of Attraction briefly back in Chapter 4. I am not a full subscriber to *The Secret* version of the Law of Attraction. The 2006 book by Rhonda Byrne sold 30 million copies globally and gathered the Law of Attraction worldwide recognition. It is in this version that Byrne alleges that simply giving something the right 'energy' is guaranteed to be effective in achieving the outcome you're looking for.

One of my core values is taking action, if you hadn't already guessed by reading this book. So the idea that you can just *think* about something, 'give it the right energy' and then magically it will land in your lap, does not sit well with me. You need to do something to see results.

However, what I experienced through taking that intentional action of writing to five people who could buy from me every day was *things happened*. Someone, or something, noticed. Energy shifted.

It was like the Universe was watching me sat there tapping out those emails, and said, "Oh I get it now . . . you want *clients, and sales.* You're stretching out of your comfort zone to make it happen. Here . . . would you like this?"

Whether it's the Law of Attraction, the Universe, God, a higher power or just sheer coincidence, I really don't care what you call it. The point is consistently taking that action, writing those emails (and doing lots of other things besides, of course), really believing all my tiny actions would work and pay off, got results. Expected and unexpected ones. Because it changed how I showed up, how I thought about myself and what actions I was willing to take.

Trust, trust, trust

Taking lots of tiny actions and believing it will pay off is a *massive* trust exercise. We've talked a lot already about building trust with your audience and potential customers. But trust in *yourself* and your ability to do this is also key.

We have to truly believe that every day we wake up and show up for our businesses, there are tens of thousands of people out there that want and need what we're offering. If you've got even a seed of doubt that anyone is listening and needs you, it will affect your ability to act. And if we're working on the basis of people needing to see you *at least* seven times? You need to have all the belief in the world to keep being there, seven times and many more.

You are creating content and showing up in the world to help those ideal customers. And they *are* watching.

They might not respond immediately. And I know that's frustrating with all the work you're putting in.

But they are watching and subconsciously those touch points are adding up.

It's important to remember they may well be watching silently. On social media, these are often people who are 'invisible' – they're called 'ghost followers' in the marketing industry.

Ghost followers, also referred to as ghosts and ghost accounts or lurkers, are **users on social media platforms who remain inactive or do not engage in activity**. They register on platforms such as Twitter and Instagram. These users follow active members, but do not partake in liking, commenting, messaging, and posting.[32]

Even though we call them 'ghosts', we must remember: they are real people. Real people with buying power.

They'll see you and your content once . . . three times, four times . . . seven times . . . ten times. But only if you're still there, still creating content and still believing.

Slowly but surely, those 'know, like and trust' factors will build. And one day, BAM! You'll say something that hits the mark so hard they feel compelled to reach out. Now is the time. They're ready for action. They want to invest.

If you keep going, it's inevitable that you'll be in their mind. You've raised your hand and been there for a long time. You need to trust that there will be a time they choose to reach out if you just keep going.

I've seen this so many times in my own business. The

number of people that say they've followed my content for months, years sometimes even, before they were ready to take the plunge and work with me makes me realise how worthwhile *all* the little steps have been.

That's not the story for everyone of course, not everyone needs years to be ready to buy (you'll be relieved to know). Sometimes you say the right thing on the right day and it's quicker than that for an ideal customer to go from stranger to buyer.

But many, I'd say most, of the people I work with, watch me over an extended period of time before they are ready to buy. And I predict it'll be the same for you too.

And realistically, the ones that buy quickly? They are looking at your back catalogue, even if it's just a quick scan. They are judging your reliability by how much you've been present *before* they landed on you.

If you look like you just sprang from nowhere, they're less likely to be convinced. All that work you do to build up content is paying dividends whether someone sees it at the moment you produce it, or at a later stage. It's genuinely an asset.

How do you keep showing up, even when it feels like no one is listening?

Hopefully by now I've fully convinced you that it is normal and necessary to keep plugging away and being present even if it feels like it's not landing with anyone.

But until that starts to pay off and you see results, how do you keep yourself going?

Here are my tips.

> **Focus on being internally motivated, not externally.** Remember that social media is designed to keep us hooked on reactions. Detach from the need for endorsement and approval from other people. Learn to bask in the satisfaction of writing a helpful blog or sending ten emails in and of itself. Find a way to reward yourself for taking that action. Don't just do things because it gets you feedback.

> **Stop obsessing about your metrics and reach.** Data is helpful to hone what you're doing. But when you're just getting started, focus on the quality and consistency of your content instead. Learn by doing and enjoy the process, not only the outcome. The doing, the process, is the bit you're in control of and ultimately all we ever have.

> **Cultivate self-belief.** What you have to offer is valuable. Spend time looking and focusing on the

people that do say you're good and helpful. Not on all the people that aren't. Head back to Chapter 3 if you need a refresher on why you're already amazing, right now.

> **Trust that people are listening and watching.**
And this is true even if they don't engage. Find some affirmations that keep reinforcing this to yourself and save them on your phone or desktop background or record yourself saying them. Try some statements such as, "Everything I do is helping my ideal customer get ready to buy." "My ideal customers are watching and they need me."

> **Accept and embrace the fact it takes time**
What is it they say? It takes ten years to become an overnight success. You need to show up if you want the same back. Make peace with the fact that putting yourself out there even when you don't get instant results is the normal run of things. You're absolutely experiencing the same as everyone else that has gone on to achieve everything they wished for. It's coming to you too.

> **Put the blinkers on and "stick to the knitting".**
Stop comparing yourself with others. Minimise, reduce, mute or block the people who make you think you're failing at this when things are slow to get started. "Stick to the knitting?" It's a phrase popularised by Tom Peters in his book, *In Search*

of Excellence, that means staying with what you know so you can build it up to be the best it can be. Don't get side-tracked. Don't spread yourself too thin. Be politely persistent and keep going.

> **Find a community of people who understand what you're doing.** Starting your own business is lonely. Working solo, as many of us will for most if not all of our business-owning careers, means it's essential to connect with others to help you on the journey. In those days, weeks and months where you're putting out content and waiting for a response from your ideal customers, find like-minded business owners and networks to keep talking to and sharing your feelings and wobbles with. There's nothing more reassuring than hearing a tonne of other business owners tell you they've been *exactly* where you are and that it all works out in the end.

"How long will it take me to start getting something back from all this work, Vicky?"

I know you're going to hate me, but there isn't a fixed answer to this question.

There are so many moving parts and elements that can affect your success and how quickly it comes to you.

But what if I were to tell you the one place to focus your efforts to get the fastest results possible . . . ?

The thing that will ultimately determine whether you see the outcome you want quickly in your business is your mindset.

It's a bit like 'you can't out train a bad diet' if we're looking for a health analogy.

All the actions and plans and blueprints and practical learning in the world can't override what your mind is saying to you.

This is where a message of pure consistency can be flawed.

I posted to my social media once 'consistency pays off' and showed my income over the period of 18 months, starting at just €241 in January 2019 to a bumper €17,000 month in June 2020.

A lot of people found it really motivating and shared comments to tell me so. "This is so inspiring! Thanks for sharing!" "This is so cool! Your honesty and humble approach is admirable! Finding this a great motivator!"

But one follower, let's call her Karen, was pretty peeved: "Got to be completely honest, I find this totally the opposite of inspiring. When things feel like a struggle and like nothing is happening, no matter how much I show up, it's incredibly demotivating and knocks my confidence . . . I don't want to show up consistently because it feels like there's no point."

We will all be there at some point on our journey, where Karen was when she wrote that comment. We will all go through periods (even when we're more 'established') where we are showing up and being 'consistent', yet feeling like nothing is paying off.

The difference between those who succeed and those who decline when hitting those periods is not a secret entrepreneur action or practical tip that everyone is keeping from you.

It's a mindset.

How you choose to *think* about what you are doing and the results you are (or aren't) seeing is key. It is what will make you someone who achieves their goal of setting up their business or the opposite, someone who fails because they haven't got their mindset straight. This is why I wrote this book for you.

Don't ask me, "What did you *do* to create a successful business?"

Ask me, "How do you *think* in order to create a successful business?"

In my own experience, when it comes to actions, I cannot tell you the amount of times that I've thought, "This is it! This will be the breakthrough! *This* email/social post/podcast appearance/article in the press/speaking gig is going to be the thing that opens the floodgates and means I'm fully booked forever."

Honestly, I'm rolling my eyes at myself writing that. You'd think I'd have learnt by now. And yeah, I get it. Some people will get lucky and get a huge boost like a TV appearance or a recommendation from a big name or a post that goes viral that 'makes' them.

But that's not frequent. It's not something that can be relied upon. And usually there's been a *huge* amount of work behind the scenes to be ready to capitalise on that once-in-a-lifetime exposure.

If not a big break, what can be relied upon to give you the success you want?

Your commitment and persistence to being present and serving your customers.

I'll finish this chapter with a story.

When I launched my first ever group programme, I was three years into business. I had a clear idea of my ideal customer and mailing list of nearly 1,000 people, an engaged social media following totalling 7K people across three platforms and a Facebook group with 600 ideal customers in it. On the surface I had all the elements to sell well.

I put a lot of work into marketing the course. I followed all my own advice. I had a waitlist of 17 people (my aim was to get 25 signed up). I released the programme to the waitlist on a Thursday evening and scheduled an email to go out to the rest of my mailing list over 1000+ on Friday morning with the link to buy.

This was going to be rip-roaring success! As I prepared everything for the launch I was remembering a podcast I'd listened to from Instagram coach Sara Tasker. Tasker had launched the first ever run of her 'Insta Retreat' programme back in 2017 and sold it out over the course of a 2-hour train journey. She popped it on sale online. Got on a train. Opened her inbox as she was about to step off the train and saw all the places were gone.

I fantasised that this would be me.

I would log in to my email inbox later on the Friday and find all of my 25 sign ups present and correct and I wouldn't have to do any more marketing. I would kick back and relax, knowing I had achieved a €20k launch and bask in my own smug satisfaction that all my marketing had worked.

Of course, that's not what happened.

Honestly, you'd think I'd have learnt by now.

After the emails went out to the waitlist and my general mailing list across Thursday and Friday morning, I logged on around midday on the Friday to see what the sales looked like. As I clicked to open my inbox I thought all 25 sign ups was probably a stretch but . . . maybe I'd have seven? Five people signed up? Even three would be nice?

What was the reality in those first hours?

One.

Sitting in my inbox was one sign up. One person I had already talked to at length and felt confident would buy.

One.

Maybe you'll read that and think, "Well, Vicky, you must be a terrible business owner then." But I want to tell you *this is the normal experience.*

I could at that point have thrown the towel in, assumed that this meant that *no one* else was going to buy my programme, hidden under the duvet and felt sorry for myself.

But I didn't. I chose what I made that figure mean.

What did I make it mean?

I made it mean that I had work to do. To explain the value of my offer. To encourage more people and answer their questions. To jump on calls with people who weren't sure. To keep marketing and talking about it and feeling confident and enthusiastic so that was conveyed to people considering buying.

I committed and remained persistent with being present and serving my customers. Knowing that my programme could *really* help people.

By the time that group programme started I had 11 sign ups. And eight of my members and clients that were going to come through the programme free of charge to help them solidify the work we were doing together. So a total of 19 people on my brand new, never-been-tried-before course.

If I'd given up when I first opened that inbox to a measly one sign up, I'd have never realised there were another ten people out there on the Internet who wanted what I had to offer.

It was a combination of the actions I took and the *way I chose to think* that got that programme filled.

Don't ask me, "What did you *do* to fill your course?"

Ask me, "How did you *think* in order to fill your course?"

How you think will determine your success.

Let's recap

1. Don't get sucked into the need for Instant Gratification, particularly with social media. Keep taking action for you and your business's long term benefit, *even if you don't see an instant reaction*.

2. No-one is an overnight success. It is *not* normal or possible for 99% of people to launch a business and be fully booked within weeks. Just the same as your clients can't suddenly be the healthy version of themselves they wish for in just a few days.

3. Harness the power of the compound effect. It's never about a single action. Or a single result. It's about all the small things you do that add up to where you want to go.

4. Trust, trust, trust. Find ways to start truly believing that every day you wake up there are tens of thousands of people out there that want and need what you're offering.

5. Your hard work will all pay off when your actions and your thoughts align. Take the steps *and* think the thoughts of a successful business owner.

Stop thinking (notice)

> No-one even liked my social media post, who's ever going to buy from me?

> What's the point, I didn't get any results last time I tried

> What am I doing wrong?

Start thinking (flip to)

> Someone is going to read this one day who really needs it

> Every little thing I do in my business is all adding up

> There are thousands of people that want what I offer – how can I serve them today?

One final story

I arrived at the foot of the ArcelorMittal Orbit and looked up. It's a 114.5-metre-high sculpture and observation tower situated in the Olympic Park in Stratford, London, and I was there to complete a challenge that had been set by my coach Julie that year.

"Do something that scares you!" she'd said to our mastermind group.

I'd agreed to give the abseil a go to push me out of my comfort zone alongside Julie and Erin, a fellow mastermind member who also happens to be my book editor now.

Together we were going to undertake the UK's highest freefall abseil. It was a beautiful sunny autumn day and we stood together at the entrance waiting for our instructors to collect us.

Signing up had been the easy bit. Julie had shared the link to book in. A couple of clicks on the website, choose the date and time, quick glance over the terms and conditions to check I'm qualified and fit enough to attempt this, add the GoPro footage to capture all the hilarity and fun, and then turn up in practical clothes on the day. Simple.

But as we stood there, the nerves started to kick in. The reality of what we were about to do, staring up at the height we were about to drop ourselves over the edge of . . . the reality didn't feel so fun anymore.

I hadn't abseiled since I was 13 on an adventure week in Cornwall at secondary school. And that was off a comparatively small cliff on the coast.

Here I was, nearly 23 years later, about to hang myself backwards off a landmark from which I could see the whole of London underneath me like a toy set. Not the same thing at all.

I had no idea what I was doing. I couldn't remember a single thing from my previous abseiling attempt as a teenager. It was all completely new and I was going to be well and truly uncomfortable – not just with the process, but the absolutely petrifying height we were doing it from.

Our instructors were warm and friendly. Enthusiastic, they kept us chatting and relaxed as we got into our helmets and harnesses and took the elevator to the top of the structure where our ropes were ready for us.

"Has anyone ever gotten to this point and not gone through with it?" I asked.

"I can only remember one guy. He was a young American who'd been out drinking the night before and had an outrageous hangover. He'd obviously never had a hangover before and couldn't work out where the headache and nausea were coming from!"

Okay. No turning back then. I couldn't be the only person alongside a teenager who couldn't handle their drink to fail to go through with this.

We were at the top.

"Vicky! Do you want to step forward first and take the ones on the right?"

Gulp. I was up.

My instructor worked methodically attaching me to the ropes and talking calmly to me, explaining exactly what everything did and how to operate the mechanism by which I could lower myself to the ground, 100-plus metres below.

I listened and tried not to get distracted by the gusts of wind, the crazy view from the open height and another fellow mastermind buddy who was filming the whole thing from inside the viewing platform, grinning and waving happily from the safety of her enclosed space.

"Just stand there . . . that's right. And position your heels just over the edge."

My body had gone into shock. This felt huge and scary. I observed the thoughts coming up in my mind.

"You don't have to do this!"

"What are you trying to prove?!"

"You've never done this before, you could get it totally wrong!"

"Holy cow, that's a long way down."

"RUN AWAAAAAAY!"

As I clung to the ropes and settled back into the harness, I reverted back to breathwork I'd been taught for pushing out my baby – deep breaths in and short, sharp breaths out. It seemed an automatic coping mechanism my body had defaulted to in order to control what could easily have turned into a wail coming out of my mouth instead, invoked by pure fear.

"Now start to lean back, feel the rope take your weight. That's it. Great job. Keep going. Keep stepping down the side. You're doing it – well done! You're my hero, Vicky!" the instructor cheered.

"You're definitely not mine right now!" I screamed back, trying to crack a joke as I slowly realised I was now hanging at 90 degrees off the sculpture, my full bodyweight in the harness, with my hands gripping the rope so tightly I could feel my pulse through my fingers.

I kept edging. I concentrated so hard on taking the tiniest steps until, all too soon, the solid steel ran out. Below was just open air. One more step and I was in total freefall.

There wasn't anywhere else to go at that point. I was committed. The only way to the bottom was to continue the descent. The worst of it was over. The starting. The gut-wrenching, body-screaming first steps to hang myself off the side. I'd begun.

I'd only really moved about one or two metres. I certainly didn't feel like an expert at this abseiling stuff. But I knew enough from those initial minutes (even if they had felt like hours) to understand the ropes were strong and I was in control of my speed.

And so I stepped. Into thin air.

My feet left the steel and I gulped as I swung under the platform, nothing supporting me apart from the harness and nothing to hold but the ropes. Dangling there waiting for the rope to stop swinging back and forth I realised . . .

I was doing it.

In the open air. Free-falling. With just a few minutes of basic skills and instructions in my head. I was using them and making it happen.

I kept edging myself down. A few centimetres at a time.

And as I did, my mind started to come onside too.

"Okay, you can keep it really slow . . . It doesn't feel too uncomfortable . . . I sort of get what I'm doing . . . This is safe for me to do . . ."

I continued.

And gradually, really gradually, I started to enjoy myself.

The breeze slowly rotated me around occasionally and gave me an incredible view over the capital, with the trains snaking below and The Shard and London Eye in the distance. By the time I was two-thirds of the way down I felt confident enough to take one of my hands off the rope and wave to my husband below.

The voice in my mind had changed.

"You did it! You're almost at the ground! It was actually quite a cool experience, wasn't it?! I'm so proud of myself! I can't wait to tell people I've done this!" it said jubilantly.

Don't get me wrong – I was slow. Really slow. Erin was strapped up to her ropes well after me, yet shot past me and got to the ground a good while before I touched down. (Editor's note: It might be of interest to know that the reason I shot past Vicky was because my hands were so numb and sore from holding on so tightly to the ropes that I felt it was safest for me to go a little faster. I also was undergoing rehab on my hip at the time, which was giving me some pain in the harness, so again, it felt safest to go a little faster. I enjoyed the view less and certainly never reached that point Vicky did where she took her hands off the ropes and trusted them to hold her as she waved at her husband! I couldn't understand – and I still can't! – how she did that. Yet another piece of proof that you can look at someone's 'fast' journey, but you never really know what's going on in their head or business.)

But I was doing it.

And as I pushed the rope through my hands, inch by inch, I started to reflect on the fact that the experience, the way I was undertaking this abseil, was a metaphor for the way I operate my business. The same way I encourage my clients to operate theirs and how I would love you to embrace running yours.

I wasn't the fastest. I doubt I was the best they'd ever seen at abseiling. It wasn't perfect. There was a *lot* of new information to take in at the beginning. A huge part of my body and mind, the parts trying to keep me safe, screamed at me not to do it.

But I pushed through to conquer it. I didn't let the negative voices in my head stop me. I listened and took action as I was told. I trusted the experts. There were moments of fear. But I took the smallest of steps and rope releases to get to where I wanted. They all added up. I did it.

Just like me abseiling that day, I felt fearful, clueless and overwhelmed when I started running my business. But by taking tiny actions, even imperfect ones, getting support and catching my negative stories and beliefs along the way, I was able to achieve something huge. Reaching the bottom of the UK's highest freefall abseil *and* running a dream business.

And so can you.

I hope you come away from this book:

> Ready to take action to build a business, even if that looks like tiny steps
> Confident to be visible and start sharing who you are and what you do with the world, knowing you're wildly capable
> Wanting to have a go at things because you understand you can't get it 'wrong' and that you'll learn and move forward with everything you try
> Knowing how to catch your own stories and negative beliefs that might otherwise undermine your actions and start to rewire your brain for more supportive, positive and abundant thinking to get the results you want

How you think will dictate the actions you choose, the products you create, the content you put out, the people you align yourself with, your ability to enthuse and excite your prospective customers, and your capacity to battle against any societal prejudices and systems that threaten to hold you back.

You are so needed. So important. So valuable. And even in those dark moments when it feels like nothing is working and you can't edge down that rope, taking even tiny steps towards your goals all adds up.

You need to just start now.

References

How to change your mindset

1. Laura Farrington – www.meditatewithlaura.ie

Chapter 1

2. Erickson Coaching International, "How to use a life wheel in coaching", https://erickson.edu/blog/solution-focused-life-coaching-wheel
3. Jodie Gale, "How to silence the inner critic by cultivating self-compassion", https://jodiegale.com/how-to-silence-the-inner-critic-by-cultivating-self-compassion

Chapter 2

4. *Lexico English Dictionary*, https://www.lexico.com/definition/scarcity
5. Ray Dodd – www.raydodd.co.uk

Chapter 3

6. Tanya Geisler as a guest on Julie Parker's *The Priestess Podcast* – https://juliesuzanneparker.com/tanyageisler
7. Tanya Geisler – https://tanyageisler.com
8. *The Cambridge Dictionary*, https://dictionary.cambridge.org/dictionary/english/infopreneur
9. Sammy – https://thenutritionalpalette.com

Chapter 4

10. Kerry Lyons – https://theimperfectlife.co
11. Adam Grant, *Think Again* (London: WH Allen, 2021). See also *Choiceology*, season 7, episode 6, June 2021: https://www.schwab.com/resource-center/insights/content/choiceology-season-7-episode-6
12. Gay Hendricks, *The Big Leap* (San Francisco: HarperOne, 2009)
13. Lucy Legal – https://www.lucylegal.co.uk
14. Neil Farber, "The truth about the Law of Attraction. It doesn't exist", https://www.psychologytoday.com/ie/blog/the-blame-game/201609/the-truth-about-the-law-attraction
15. Ann Pietrangelo, "What the Baader-Meinhof Phenomenon Is and Why You May See It Again . . . and Again" https://www.healthline.com/health/baader-meinhof-phenomenon#what-it-is
16. Reid Hoffman – https://www.businessinsider.com/the-iterate-fast-and-release-often-philosophy-of-entrepreneurship-2009-11?r=US&IR=T

Chapter 5

17. Charlotte Stirling Reed – https://www.srnutrition.co.uk
18. Eve Kalinik – https://evekalinik.com
19. Sandra Greenbank – https://sandragreenbank.com
20. Lucy Green – https://lucygreen.net

Chapter 6

21. Henrietta Onwuegbuzie, *Is making an impact the path to profit?*, https://insights.som.yale.edu/insights/is-making-an-impact-the-path-to-profit, May 2019

Chapter 7

22. Helen, The Tummy Whisperer, https://www.thetummy-whisperer.co.uk
23. Dotti Balhatchet, www.instagram.com/p/CP59iYCLdFI

24. Vogue Williams, www.thesun.ie/fabulous/6797679/i-hid-my-quick-post-baby-weight-loss-vogue-williams/
25. Nicola Rae-Wickham – www.alifemoreinspired.com

Chapter 8

26. Rachel Maunder, Story Coach – www.rachelmaunder.com
27. Paul Zak, *How stories change the brain*, https://greater-good.berkeley.edu/article/item/how_stories_change_brain, Dec 2013
28. Brené Brown, *Unlocking Us Podcast*, https://brenebrown.com/podcast/brene-on-comparative-suffering-the-50-50-myth-and-settling-the-ball/, March 2020
29. Deloitte Digital, *Trust drives profitable pricing* https://www.deloittedigital.com/content/dam/deloittedigital/us/documents/offerings/offering-20210125-hxiu-pricing.pdf

Chapter 9

30. Deloitte Digital, *Trust drives profitable pricing*
31. Jen Carrington, "Make it Happen Podcast", https://www.jencarrington.com/make-it-happen-a-podcast-for-bloggers-and-creatives/2017/5/16/living-and-working-in-seasons, May 2017

Chapter 10

32. https://en.wikipedia.org/wiki/Ghost_followers

Recommended Resources

People I love, books I've read, podcasts I've listened to, apps I've used and courses I've taken to build my entrepreneur mindset.

Meditation and mindfulness resources
Meditate with Laura – https://www.meditatewithlaura.ie
Eckhart Tolle, *The Power of Now* (California: New World Library, 1999)

Apps for meditation
Headspace – https://www.headspace.com
Insight Timer – https://insighttimer.com
Chopra Center – https://chopra.com/app

Apps for affirmations
Clementine – https://clementineapp.com
I Am – https://apps.apple.com/us/app/i-am-daily-affirmations/id874656917

Money mindset resources
Kate Northrup, *Money A Love Story* (London: Hay House, 2009)

Jen Sincero, *You Are A Badass At Making Money* (London:
  John Murray Learning, 2018)
Sarah Akwisombe, *The Money Is Coming* (London:
  Piatkus, 2020)
Jen McFarlane, The Money Medium –
  https://themoneymedium.com
Ray Dodd, Money coach and mentor –
  https://www.raydodd.co.uk

Anti-racism resources
Nova Reid, *The Good Ally* (London: HQ, 2021)
Reni Eddo-Lodge, *Why I'm No Longer Talking To White
  People About Race* (London: Bloomsbury, 2018)
Be Antiracist with Ibram X Kendi Podcast
  www.ibramxkendi.com/be-antiracist-podcast
About Race with Reni Eddo-Lodge www.aboutracepodcast.com
The 1619 Project – www.nytimes.com/interactive/
  2019/08/14/magazine/1619-america-slavery.html
Nova Reid's Anti-racism course – https://novareid.com/
  services/anti-racism-course/
Just Start Now podcast, 'How to encourage diversity in the
  wellness industry with Toral Shah' –
  https://vickyshilling.com/just-start-now-podcast/006-
  how-to-encourage-equality-and-diversity-in-your-wellness-
  business-with-toral-shah

LGBTQ+ resources
Sarah Taylor – https://sarah-taylor.co.uk
Sarah Taylor, *The LGBTQ Inclusion Guide* – https://
  thequeerpreneur.lpages.co/lgbtq-inclusion-guide
Just Start Now podcast, 'How to make your wellness
  business more inclusive with Sarah Taylor' – https://
  vickyshilling.com/just-start-now-podcast/how-to-make-
  your-wellness-business-more-inclusive-with-sarah-taylor

Acknowledgements

A book takes time and commitment, and that space could not have been created without the support and love of my husband David who tolerated me writing late into the night week after week to get this published and did more than his fair share of chores and childcare while this other 'baby' of mine was coming in to the world. I would not be where I am, nor have the business I have, without his encouragement and grounding.

A big thank you to the BETA readers who read through the very first draft of this book and gave me such careful feedback: Rose, Rachel, Sammy, Birdy and Marian.

A massive thank you to my editor and book mentor Erin Chamberlain who helped me through the whole book writing process, to shape and draw out the words and coaxed me into including more stories of my own experiences throughout these pages. Without her, this book would not be in your hands.

And finally, to my clients. Each and every one of you inspires me and fills me with ideas that get me up every morning, creating content just for you. Keep being amazing at what you do, I'll be right here figuring out how to help you best.

Index

Vicky Shilling is a business mentor, speaker, podcaster and sometime lecturer on online business growth. Originally from Kent in the United Kingdom, she left in 2017 to be with an Irish man who wouldn't leave Ireland and now lives in Dublin with her husband and daughter Oonagh. When she is not working with clients or creating content, Vicky can be found in the kitchen not following recipes, at the gym lifting weights or exploring Ireland for its best pubs and seafood.

Don't forget to check out **vickyshilling.com** for:
> Book resources
> Blog posts
> Latest podcast episodes
> Upcoming events
> More details on mentoring and the Just Start Now course and community

I'd love to hear how you just start now after reading this book. Let me know at:
hi@vickyshilling.com
@vicky.shilling (Instagram)

CPSIA information can be obtained
at www.ICGtesting.com
Printed in the USA
LVHW050815090322
712947LV00015B/495

9 781739 892500